Light On the Dark Side Of God

By M. M. Campbell
3d ed.

Light
On the
Dark Side
Of God

M. M.Campbell
3d ed.

©1989-2019 MMC
All Rights Reserved

Available at:
http://www.The-Character-of-God.com

ISBN 978-1-7324842-0-7

Edited by Floyd Phillips
Supplemental Content by Kevin Straub
Cover Design by Ed Guthro
Cover Art by Darrel Tank

Printed In USA

Dedicated To
God's Invisible Church on Earth

*"The anger of the Lord will not turn back until He has
executed and performed the thoughts of His heart.
In the latter days you will understand it perfectly."
(Jeremiah 23:20; 30:23, 24)*

TABLE OF CONTENTS

Introduction

"For the Lord will rise up as on Mount Perazim, He will rage as in the valley of Gibeon; To do his deed— strange is his deed! And to work his work—alien is his work!" (Isaiah 28:21, NRSV)

We have all seen optical illusions. A familiar one looks like a picture of a vase to some people.But others see in the dark background instead, two profiles facing each other in silhouette. Behold God taking vengeance on Sodom and Gomorrah; drowning the people of Noah's time; burning the lost of all the ages. Now compare those events with the compassionate character of Jesus, who refused to hurt His enemies. They should match, according to Scripture. But do they? Is it possible we are looking at an optical illusion?

Why This Book?
Light On the Dark Side of God is offered to address these questions and comes to you in the hope of clarifying a subject that has long confused the body of Christ. Christians are clear about the gospel, that God sent His precious Son to redeem us and demonstrate the depths of His eternal love for us. God's character, as it relates to our redemption, is presented with great sensitivity and wisdom. But what has not been so clear is the issue of God's character as it relates to other things, for instance, to final things— What is the fate of those who do not choose God? Why would such a loving God, as His advocates present Him, burn the lost for eternity, when punishment at that time has no redemptive purpose, when it is administered after all minds are made up? How do God's actions then reveal the greatest Lover in the universe, while He consciously burns those who have the misfortune to be "lost"? All this while assuring us that "God is light and in Him is no darkness at all."[1]

---

[1] 1 John 1:5, NKJV.

Added to this is the enormous confusion about events of the Old Testament that make God look like a killer. Besides Noah's flood and Sodom and Gomorrah, there are many more examples: Warring with the Philistines,[2] conquering the Canaanites,[3] ordering Saul to commit genocide on the Amalekites.[4] This has looked like God's dark side to many. How can Scripture assert that He has no dark side at all? Many have found this contrast very confusing.

Due to such texts as these many believers cannot shake the suspicion that Christianity has embraced an illusion regarding the character of God—in particular the side having to do with His justice, which means, in our traditional way of thinking, making punishment fit the crime. These thoughtful students of Scripture have explored some of the questions inherent in the traditional picture of a destroying God with the result that a whole new perspective of what constitutes His "wrath" is now emerging, fully harmonious with both Scripture and the gentle character of Christ. This new perspective does not claim to exempt sinners from the consequences of a life of sin but merely expands our understanding of the mechanism by which the wages of sin are paid. That new view is the subject of this work.

Christianity, deeply rooted in Judaism and for two thousand years anticipating Christ's return in glory, has a growing credibility problem that deepens with each passing year our Lord fails to fulfill His promise to return. Some have even declared our times "the post-Christian era." In spite of exponential growth in the number of existing Christian churches and ministries; in spite of many Christians venturing forth to preach the gospel; in spite of oceans of donations from sincere believers funding this activity, this sin-cursed earth remains and Christ has not returned to end the reign of sin. This is a serious problem. Surely, the fault cannot be in Him. Could it be in us? Could there be something we're not yet seeing?

The continuing reign of sin combined with other factors raises questions about Christianity's ability to survive into the coming years as a viable life philosophy for reasonable men and women. Some suspect that God is dead; science in general thinks it has defeated the Bible; the gap widens between conservatives (generally Bible-believers) and liberals

---

[2] 1 Samuel 5.

[3] Joshua 12.

[4] 1 Samuel 15:3

(generally not).

How like God to let matters go almost to the point of hopelessness and then (to borrow from the language of gaming) to play His final trump card and take the whole pot, as a startled world looks on. Is there a surprise, so great, so amazing, that will bring back the glory God intended Christianity to be for all people?

Who needs this book? Thinking men and women everywhere, especially those who have rejected Christianity, because they have observed the very problems in Christian thought this book addresses. If you reject a God who burns the lost for eternity, this book is for you. If you have come to Christ recognizing Him as the One who invented total other-centered love (perhaps in spite of the enigma of presuming that in the end He will burn his enemies), then this work may bring you enormous relief. If you have received without question the concept of God's burning His own children—if that seems all right to you, you're in for a real eye-opener. If you are one who has never understood how the gospel works, this book is for you!

A Savior Across the Boundaries

God has seen fit to connect the history of truth with the history of Israel. It is therefore impossible to examine Biblical truth and ignore this ancient people, particularly when Scripture holds them up as an example for our times.[5] Given our vital modern concern for tolerance, I hesitate to depict Israel in less than flattering terms and would never do so, except for the very plain statements of Scripture.

We can agree, I am sure, that ancient Israel's history pertains not to that nation alone but to Christianity as well. Whatever is said of her is part of our own spiritual heritage. Nothing within this work should be construed as anything but an effort to take the history left for us in Scripture and to use it for its intended purpose of providing eternal, spiritual lessons. Christ came to "break down the middle wall of division between us, having abolished in His flesh the enmity . . . so as to create in Himself one new man from the two, thus making peace."[6] The truth of God levels out the playing field for all humans; He is an equal opportunity Savior.

---

[5] See 1 Corinthians 10:11.
[6] Ephesians 2:14, 15, NKJV.3

3

Therefore, ideally, let us take down the barriers that divide us and for a moment in time fix our eyes upon the Lamb slain from the foundation of the world. We may find in that view a far better God than tradition has given us.

God of the Old Testament

Jesus was, in fact, the God of the Old Testament,[7] a position far more believable now than in the past in light of this emerging new revelation of God. Whenever His Father appears in the sacred record, He is usually described *in the text* in order to prevent any identification errors.[8] It is important to understand that Jesus, the Old Testament God who taught Israel, could not always instruct them as he would ideally have liked due to their slowness of heart.[9] The net result has been a distortion of our perceptions of Deity. My prayer is that in this book, readers may discover a new harmony between the character of the great "I Am" as the Old Testament presents Him, and that of Christ as the gospels present Him—a harmony in favor of the compassionate character of our Lord Jesus Christ.

Mysteries Solved!

This new view of God illuminates many questions that have puzzled the world through the centuries, including the mystery of human suffering such as experienced by Job, Jesus, John the Baptist, and many other martyrs through the ages. We cannot necessarily know the reasons for the suffering of others, but in light of this new understanding of God we may be able to learn more about the "whys" of our own suffering.

Is it a result of the *rule* that we get the master we choose to obey—either God, the good Master; or Satan, the destroyer? Is it the *exception that proves the rule*, which I call "The Job Syndrome"? Or are we looking at other underlying principles manifesting in adversity?

Other works have been and will continue to be published on this topic. Interested Bible students will want to consider the broad range of thinking from various sources regarding God's character since all commentators do not see the matter (or say it) exactly alike. However, I must at this point

---

[7] John 5:39. See also Proverbs 30:4; Psalm 2:12; Ezekiel 21:10; 1 Corinthians 10:4, etc.

[8] I.e., Genesis 1:1; Daniel 7:9, 10, etc.

[9] See, for example, Ezekiel 20:25, 26; Matthew 5:21, 22, 27, 28, 33-37.

interject a note of caution regarding the efforts of some to take this new view of God in the direction of universalism, which says that all will at last be saved—a direction in which I and many other responsible supporters of this view affirm it clearly does not go. While on the surface universalism may appear to be an admirable improvement over dark views of God's character that have caused so much damage throughout history, within it is a danger of discounting the natural results of sin and its permanent affect on the human soul if not eradicated. Thus in adopting this view as an alternative to the damaging lies about God found in mainstream religion, many are led into imagining that since God is not our problem we may indulge in the pleasures of sin now and still escape its deadly effects in eternity. This is a most subtle enticement of the enemy designed to seduce us into complacency while we ignore the only remedy provided through Christ to prepare us to live in the presence of God.

The Landscape of Divine Punishment
This book examines the confusing landscape of divine punishment. Many atheists have called our attention to what objective minds might term "inconsistencies" in the picture of God Christianity has offered the world. We have generally responded with what I now call the "eight hundred pound gorilla" theory of God. Where does the eight hundred pound gorilla sleep? Anywhere he wants. This is what is commonly taught in religion as "the sovereignty of God."

Our God, though omnipotent, is not like an eight hundred pound gorilla. Because God is love, popular opinion tries to serve up the concept that burning humans for eternity is the most loving thing that a loving God can do. Many see through this charade and say that the burning of humans alive is evil. After all, did not God express this opinion many times in the Old Testament in connection with Israel burning their children in sacrificing them to Molech? Contrary to popular opinion, in exercising His sovereignty God does not do anything and everything He has power to do. He must make sense. He must be consistent with those qualities of character that are in Him. And where the wages of sin are experienced, His actions must pass the scrutiny of those He desires to save. It must meet the standards of both mercy and justice (rightly understood) in order to appeal to reasonable minds. His ways must recommend themselves not just to humans but to holy angels as well. After all, what happens to humans could happen to them. How can the universe be secure from another outbreak of sin, unless heaven's inhabitants are fully persuaded that God's ways are right and find His ways worthy of glory, honor and praise? As the universe watches the sin problem and observes how God resolves it through to its full conclusion at last, the methods He chooses to use will determine whether or not there will be any doubts or leftover fear that could seed another rebellion.

Mercy and Justice

Justice is an issue whose sinister seeds have produced fear and doubt in the minds of humans and angels alike. Since Lucifer first insisted that true justice requires punishment for infractions of law, thus making it incompatible with mercy, fear has resulted. And the presence of fear prevents humans from experiencing perfect love, the very essence of God's character and the motivation on which all creation is designed to thrive. John makes clear that perfect or mature love expels all fear and that fear has to do with punishment.

If Lucifer's allegations were true and every sin must be punished, then fear would be part of God's normal government and love would not be His essence. But God is love and Satan is a liar and father of liars; therefore, what we need is a corrected understanding of God's kind of justice that does not destroy mercy. In fact, when the truth finally emerges we see that mercy and true justice actually complement and do not contradict at all, as we have assumed.

Because righteousness is not *primarily* about law-keeping but about living in harmony and fellowship with God and His children, sin is an issue of broken relationships rather than infractions of rules. Breaking laws merely indicates distrust of God and can never be resolved until restoration of full trust. Were God to rely on threats of punishment, as most people assume He does to compel people into obedience to His laws, then fear would be part of His methods and John would be incorrect in telling us that love and fear are incompatible.

Earthly governments with their many methods to control and maintain order do not provide an accurate picture of Biblical justice. Scripture reveals that *heavenly justice restores everything and everyone back to the original design*. It restores relationships, recovers what has been broken or lost, reconciles humans back into fellowship with Him. It has nothing to do with God's inflicting harm on those who defy His authority, though clearly it does involve releasing people from His protection when they demand to no longer live under His shelter and authority.

Justice from heaven's perspective is really God allowing people to have what they ultimately choose for their lives, even when that end will be tragic. But God desires that everyone be restored to wholeness, and this is the sole design for both biblical justice and mercy.

Mercy, another name for grace, describes God's intrinsic nature. God is merciful, gracious, kind, and patient and all of these qualities make up facets of the love by which He is known. Properly understood, justice—God seeking to restore everything back to His original purpose—is also a facet of His love. Punishment has no part in heavenly justice except when the term describes people suffering the natural ill-effects of insisting on going their own way apart from God. We will unpack this more clearly as we move through this and other related issues in this book.

Come, Let Us Reason

As Christians, should we care what happens to the lost? It shouldn't affect us or those we love, right? Yet how can we be sure? It will certainly affect someone's loved ones. Is there a danger that we might imagine ourselves so special as to be aloof from sin's natural effects on our world? "Enter by the narrow gate; for wide is the gate and broad is the way that leads to destruction, and there are many who go in by it. Because narrow is the gate and difficult is the way which leads to life, and there are few who find it."[10]

A Range of Gospel Topics

This work covers a lot of ground. While Christian writers usually focus one work on a single spiritual theme; such as prayer, faith, death, or science and the Bible, that is not the case with this book. It takes a number of pillars to uphold a correct appreciation of God's true character of love. Therefore, in order to present this new perspective, it is necessary to discuss, briefly, a range of interlocking gospel subjects that contribute to a clearer revelation of God. Thus you will find a more exhaustive presentation of each of these subjects in other works.

---

[10] Matthew 7:13, 14, NKJV.

[11] Jeremiah 29:13, NKJV.

Yet each of these points support the main theme which we shall explore to its depths. "[Y]ou will seek Me and find Me, when you search for Me with all your heart."[11] Truth does not usually lie on Scripture's surface, and definitions need to be derived from Scripture itself, not from presumptions or traditional interpretations. Conclusions must take into account the full range of Scriptural statements on a topic, and those desiring truth regarding God's character must be interested enough and willing to examine that full Scriptural range. This will become more apparent as we take up this exciting study of God's character. "[H]e who comes to God must believe that he exists, and that he is a rewarder of those who seek him."[12]

Can you imagine the possibility of serving God solely because you admire Him? It is actually possible to come to see nothing in Him that is arbitrary or mean-spirited, nothing harmful to us or to anyone. He can make sense at last. Imagine not having to tolerate in our view of Him anything we would not applaud in each other. Imagine our obedience and service flowing spontaneously out of genuine appreciation and respect for who He really is—a consistently gracious, forgiving, and always loving Father. Heaven would then no longer be viewed as a fire escape. It would be a place we want to go to be with the God we admire and love so much. "There is no fear in love; but perfect love casts out fear."[13] Imagine discovering a God we can not only love, but whom we can *like* even more. It is my desire and joy to introduce you to just such a God.

The Vindication of God

One may surmise that somewhere, in the far reaches of the past, God's intelligent creation lived in the secure embrace of His character of love. No doubt existed to make them uneasy; no foreboding disturbed their peace of mind. But it became someone's desire to alienate others' affections and steal their trust from Him through lies and subtle insinuation, which continued on through future years, becoming more venerated as they gathered age. Until now our Creator has carried the burden of those lies and insinuations. While multitudes believe that under certain circumstances, turmoil and violence are necessary and the

---

[12] Hebrews 11:6, WEB.

[13] 1 John 4:18, NKJV.

8

most loving thing God can do, many more react by rejecting the wonderful God who loves them and wants only their good. As a result, confusion prevails. We look at this apparent darkness in God, and we wonder. There really is light on what before we could only perceive as darkness. Has God held the best news about His character until the end? On the other hand, if you're looking for excuses to continue in sin, you won't find them here.

May God guide you, as you consider Him in a beautiful new way. "Prove all things; hold fast that which is good."[14]

---

[14] 1 Thessalonians 5:21, KJV.

1

Our Misunderstood God

*"[T]he earth shall be full of
the knowledge of the Lord
[a]s the waters cover the sea."
(Isaiah 11: 9, NKJV).*

Years ago a realtor showed me a house as a possible purchase. It was a "fixer-upper," modestly priced, boasting a glorious eastern view from the large living room window. Rich dark grass and the thick hanging foliage of shade trees and ornamental bushes stretched out toward a patchwork valley floor, which faded into blue hills far in the distance. The view was everything the realtor said—from that direction. But he didn't say much about the back yard, set up against a rail fence that surrounded the local stockyards. Only a salesman could evaluate that house without reference to the back yard. When my thoughts turn to the Being we call "God," I remember that house, for there is also a wondrously strange side to our traditional view of God—a side that seems dark to us at times, a perplexing side taught from many pulpits today, a side that has puzzled and even distressed thoughtful men and women for centuries, perhaps for millennia.

Sinners In the Hands of an Angry God
In colonial America a Massachusetts minister named Jonathan Edwards, appalled at the worldliness creeping into his church, warned his parishioners of the fate awaiting them if they continued in their unrepentant ways. No one since has described it better than he in his historic sermon, "Sinners in the Hands of an Angry God":

The God that holds you over the pit of hell, much as one holds a spider, or some loathsome insect, over the fire, abhors you, and is dreadfully provoked; his wrath towards you burns like fire; he looks upon you as worthy of nothing else, but to be cast into the fire; he is of purer eyes than to bear to have you in his sight; you are ten thousand times more abominable in his eyes, as the most hateful and venomous serpent is in ours. You have offended him infinitely more than ever a stubborn rebel did his prince: and yet it is nothing but his hand that holds you from falling into the fire every moment: it is ascribed to nothing else, that you did not go to hell the last night; that you was [sic] suffered to awake again in this world, after you closed your eyes to sleep; and there is no other reason to be given, why you have not dropped into hell since you arose in the morning, but that God's hand has held you up: there is no other reason to be given why you have not gone to hell, since you have sat here in the house of God, provoking his pure eyes by your sinful wicked manner of attending his solemn worship: yea, there is nothing else that is to be given as a reason why you do not at this very moment drop down into hell.. . .

Edwards so moved his congregation with his description of God's wrath and the tortures of the damned, he sparked a revival known to history as the first Great Awakening. Such is the power of a sermon well prepared. What would evangelists do without the popular doctrine of eternally burning hell? Maybe it is time to reexamine some of the presumptions that make this popular doctrine so central in modern Christianity.

Responses to an idea such as Edwards expressed span the breadth of human emotion. Some initiate and maintain church connection more to avoid this fiery fate than for any other reason, while others would not come near a community espousing such a concept. Because that is the apparent message of Scripture, Christians, drawn by the love of God displayed at Calvary, conclude it must be okay if that's what He wants to do. After all, the wicked must be punished, they assume. Yet their moral compass malfunctions at this point. Instead of saying, "There's something wrong here" and praying through intense Bible study to understand what the real truth might be, perceiving that the same mind that conceived the plan of salvation in love for all mankind, could not also manufacture such horror, they take the easy way, relying on the excuse that this is what Christendom has "always" believed, isn't it?

Ethical Problems

Despite the seemingly clear way in which Jesus represents Himself, the traditional view of Christianity's God is heavy with ethical problems that have puzzled reasonable men and women since time began. As long as humans have reasoned on the subject of God, they have wondered about His apparently destructive side. Noah's flood, Sodom and Gomorrah, eternal hell fire....How can a God who punishes so cruelly also say: "I have no pleasure in the death of the wicked, but that the wicked turn from his way and live. Turn, turn from your evil ways! For why should you die?"[1]

"How can I give you up, Ephraim? How can I hand you over, Israel? ...My heart churns within Me; My sympathy is stirred." "My heart sobs like a flute for Moab, sobs like a flute for the men of Kirheres; that accumulated treasure all lost."[2]

Would not humans manifesting this personality split be considered psychotic? How amazing that decent men and women of Christian faith could accept so casually what the non-Christian world finds shocking and cruel. Remember, God is not amoral like an eight hundred pound gorilla. He doesn't always act simply because He has the power to act. He wants us to understand the truth about this presumed aspect of His character. There is so much more to know than we have thought or presumed in the past.

The story of the cross has tremendous drawing power on the hearts and lives of humanity. What God did for us at Calvary will be the subject of praise from His creatures throughout eternity, for it cost Him so much and exceeds the far limits of our concepts of mercy. Yet the story of the cross has acquired the "drag" of a concept of God's vengeance that fails to reach the level of even human justice. From our perspective, punishment must always fit the crime, even and especially where God exercises justice in His universe. Yet the mainstream version of "the gospel" contradicts a true understanding of love as taught by Jesus and His disciples.

How can God exercise such "cruel and unusual" punishment as drowning the entire world or burning whole cities and all the humans in them and yet still be considered loving and just as He and we Christians claim? He went all the way to Calvary to preserve our freedom of choice.

---

[1] Ezekiel 33:11, NKJV.

[2] Hosea 11:8, NKJV; Jeremiah 48:36, JB.

12

Yet is choice really free if God stands over us threatening to destroy us if we choose wrong? After enduring the cross at the hands of sinners to redeem humanity, thus demonstrating His unchangeable love before the universe, why would He, in the end, contradict that demonstration by executing those who choose to spurn Him?

How can a God who kills command His people not to kill—and yet still expect them to be transformed into His likeness? How does the mild and gentle Jesus reflect the character of the "fire-breathing" Old Testament God He came more fully to reveal? There may be nothing that has contributed more to the advancement of atheism than the contradictory explanations given for these perplexing unanswered questions about Christianity.

The 19th century skeptic, Robert G. Ingersoll, spoke for multitudes through the ages when he addressed the idea of an eternally burning hell in these words: "Infinite punishment is infinite cruelty, endless injustice, immortal meanness…

"Christians have placed upon the throne of the universe a God of eternal hate. I cannot worship a being whose vengeance is boundless, whose cruelty shoreless, and whose malice is increased by the agonies he inflicts."[3] Atheists represent an entire community of souls for whom Jesus died, a community lost to the gospel unless we can come up with better answers to their questions than we have offered in the past. They can see through the shallowness of traditional Christian illogic and expect us to come up with something more reasonable that makes better sense. Our answers must make sense for them and still be Scriptural. Brothers and sisters, the real truth can do that! But it will require that we be willing to reexamine our assumptions about the meaning of many religious words such as redemption, gospel, justice, sin and even love itself.

Those who believe in the same toasty hell fire but assert smugly that the consuming fire eventually burns out still must contend with the contradiction that an all-wise God, who is said to be more loving than any human and who had nothing to do with originating sin or its consequences, could find no better way to dispose of sin than to burn and torture sinners alive, even for a limited time and even though they are His children still— the creation of His own hand. If burning humans alive is evil in this world for humans to do, then would it not be just as evil an act for God to do as

---

[3]"The Great Infidels," 1881.

for anyone else? Remember, simply because He has the *power* to do an act doesn't mean He has the will or that He is compelled to do it. He is always consistent with His own loving character and there are some acts that are simply contradictory to His nature. Evil is evil because it is evil. God's alleged participation in it does not somehow sanctify or excuse it. The idea of hell fire, to many, constitutes a huge "black hole" in Christianity's system of belief.

Is There Any Word From the Lord?

The past century has seen almost miraculous advances in knowledge.[4] The fields of science, medicine, and technology have introduced amazing innovations, many now several generation deep. Yet until recently that growth in knowledge has not extended to a more enlightened understanding of the word of God. Christianity has slumbered along, content with its own generally unchallenged orthodoxy while the world enters the twenty-first century. At this point God's invisible church has good reason to gaze heavenward and ask, "Is there any word from the Lord?"[5] The questions posed above have weighed down God's church from eons of ages past. As archeology slowly but increasingly confirms the Bible, should we not also see an improvement in our own knowledge of the God of the Bible? Should not these troubling questions find better answers from the word itself, through determined, prayerful efforts of earnest Biblical scholars?

Thus says the Lord:

> *Let not the wise man glory in his wisdom,*
> *Let not the mighty man glory in his might,*
> *Nor let the rich man glory in his riches: But*
> *let him who glories glory in this,*
> *That he understands and knows Me,*
> *That I am the Lord, exercising*
> *Lovingkindness, judgment, and*
> *Righteousness in the earth*
> *For in these I delight.*[6]

---

[4] See Daniel 12:4.

[5] Jeremiah 37:17, NKJV.

[6] Jeremiah 9:23, 24, NKJV.

Our Misunderstood God

Some humans are terrified to question God; they insist that the Bible record is too clear to doubt and that God punishes because He must. Only as the hand of God personally strikes, they claim, can harmony reign in the social order. After all, who wants to live in a world overrun with crime and evil, where no barriers of fear of impending judgment impede sin's onward march? This, they insist, is justice. And without justice executing judgments on offenders of its laws, no government can last. Without question Scripture speaks of judgment. "The wages of sin is death,"[7] and no place in the pages of *this* work will you read otherwise.

On the other hand there are questions screaming to be acknowledged and addressed—questions like 'What is judgment?' and 'Who is it that pays out the wages of sin?' At the same time a voice can be heard in Scripture revealing God Himself, in essence, crying out to be known and understood. So if the surface view is all-sufficient, why would we find Him pleading, "Behold Me, behold Me?"[8] Why would He encourage us to come and reason with Him?[9] Why would He direct His people to "Lift up your voice with strength; Lift it up, be not afraid; Say to the cities of Judah; Behold your God!"[10]

A terrible situation existed in ancient Israel in the time of the prophets. The writings of the contemporaries Hosea, Isaiah, Amos and Micah all reflect the religious intensity of the times.[11] Yet God declared through Hosea, "[T]he Lord brings a charge against the inhabitants of the land: 'There is no truth or mercy or knowledge of God in the land."[12] The people were "destroyed for lack" of it.[13] With all their religious fervor, they failed to pursue an accurate understanding of the God they claimed to worship, and as a result their ignorance unfolded into wholesale sin and consequent vulnerability to attacks by surrounding nations. There should be an urgency about seeking accuracy in our knowledge of God that brings about right-doing, protection, power and blessings into our lives. These are not God's arbitrary decrees as we shall discover; rather they are the underlying principles that govern the realities of daily living on this planet.

---

[7] Romans 6:23, KJV.

[8] Isaiah 65:1, KJV.

[9] Isaiah 1:18.

[10] Isaiah 40:9, NKJV.

[11] See Hosea 4:13; Isaiah 1:10-17; Amos 5:21-24; Micah 6:6-8.

[12] Hosea 4:1, NKJV.

[13] Hosea 4:6, NKJV.

We assume that we can see ancient Israel's failures clearly, yet is it possible that we have the same blinders on today but do not know it? Might our own picture of God be suspect? Every element of our theology—our religious belief systems—ultimately express how we view God: life after death, the rapture/second coming, prophecy, eternal reward and punishment, the meaning of faith—the list goes on and on.

For an enlightening eye-opener, list the various points of your personal religious belief system and then carefully analyze each one in terms of what it says about God. Is your God reasonable, fair, loving, consistent? If you find yourself asking, "Why would He do that? Why would He think that way," your view of God may be part of the problem. Then ask yourself, who is the focus of these beliefs—God or myself? In actual fact, God is consummately reasonable as Bible prophets present Him, and He pleads for humans to relate to Him at that level.[14] In its emphasis on obtaining a knowledge of God, really coming to know Him, heaven is trying to reveal to us something very important. Let's not be so quick to conclude we already understand everything, thinking we already have the truth.

Isaiah 5:12-13 speaks of humans who "do not regard the work of the Lord, nor consider the operation of His hands. [They don't understand Him?] Therefore my people have gone into captivity, because they have no knowledge" [of God's character and purposes?].[15] This seems to suggest a people who don't care to study God, because they assume they already know about Him, while, conversely, they don't know anything about Him and go into captivity because of it.

"Come now, and let us reason together, says the Lord"; "Let us pursue the knowledge of the Lord."[16] He invites discussion. He wants humans to take Him seriously and is willing to meet with us at every point of confusion, assuring us that He will not reject our sincere questions.

The New Testament asserts perhaps even more strongly our need to pursue a better understanding of our Creator. God has given us powerful resources to enhance our spiritual journey. In a text familiar to most Christians is a relevant and illuminating phrase. "[T]he weapons of our

---

[14] Isaiah 1:18.

[15] NKJV.

[16] Isaiah 1:18, NKJV; Hosea 6:3, NKJV.

warfare are not carnal but mighty in God for pulling down of strongholds; casting down arguments and every high thing that exalts itself against the knowledge of God."[17] What do our spiritual weapons cast down? Strongholds. Arguments. High things. All things, in fact, that interfere with a true knowledge of God. Is this text saying to us that an accurate knowledge of God is among the last things His enemy would have us know? Perhaps we should question why.

Ephesians 4:13 predicts a time when God's invisible church will come together in "unity of the faith and the knowledge of the Son of God."[18] Does this hint of a misunderstanding regarding the character of Deity, a misunderstanding soon to be clarified?

Hebrews says that God's chosen "always go astray in their heart, and they have not known My ways."[19] This thought recurs throughout the word.

"[T]his is eternal life," Jesus prayed, "that they may know You [God the Father], the only true God, and Jesus Christ whom You have sent."[20] Do we truly know God, as it is our privilege to know Him? as, in fact, we must know Him, if we would enter into life?

When sin fades into history at last, God's people "shall not hurt nor destroy" in the kingdom made new. Why? Because they ever live in fear of punishment? Not at all. It will be because "the earth shall be full of the knowledge of the Lord as the waters cover the sea."[21] I have counted no less than twenty-three Biblical entries specifically directing us to come to a "knowledge" of God, and likely many more exist. Scripture is clear; we have misunderstood God. He desires to be known and has instructed us to make His character our study.

God's Character In His People

It was so important to God to be understood that He sent His own Son to accurately reveal Him. We usually think of Christ as coming to save humans by offering Himself as a ransom for sin. While that is technically true, it is important to know the real meaning and context of the concept of ransom. And it is at least equally important, yet too often overlooked,

---

[17] 2 Corinthians 10:4, 5, KJV, emphasis supplied.

[18] NKJV, emphasis supplied.

[19] 3:10, NKJV.

[20] John 17:3, NKJV.

[21] Isaiah 11:9, NKJV.

that He also came to reveal His Father's character to both a fallen human race as well as the onlooking universe. Through his life example and teaching He underscored the need for humans to know God accurately. Why would that need exist, if the world already understood?

The majority rejected Jesus, largely because they did not recognize His Father in Him. They wanted a replica of their view of the Old Testament God of war, who would free their nation from its humiliating bondage to the empire of Rome. But that is not what He offered them. He brought them an invitation to come into a Kingdom that resides in a converted heart, an opportunity to reflect the true God to their enemies as well as to their friends. But their preconceived ideas rose like great barriers of granite around their hearts through which He could not reach them. Even His disciples sank beneath the crushing disappointment of the cross and did not understand until after the resurrection the true meaning of His mission. And after they understood they found it hard to shake the old paradigm of Jesus' ruling over an earthly empire in which they could rule over their enemies.

To this day the Judeo-Christian tradition has not reconciled the contrast between God as the Old Testament seems to present Him, and God the loving Father as Christ presents Him in the New Testament. Christendom is still conflicted over which view of God we ought to follow—the nonviolent character of the New Testament Jesus or the apparently armed and dangerous God of the Old Testament. It was because of this that Christ was vilified throughout His ministry and finally crucified as an impostor. Yet we still face similar questions today regarding the contrast in character between Jesus and the sometimes seemingly brutal Old Testament God He came more fully to reveal. Yet would we recognize our Lord today any better than did the Jews so long ago?

Scripture further says that God intends to reproduce His character in every human who agrees to be so molded. Yet that transformation can be inhibited when humans entertain misapprehensions about what constitutes God's character. Whether we acknowledge it or not, our characters are largely shaped by our beliefs regarding God. In fact, that may be the single most powerful factor in shaping us into who we become. From the atheist or agnostic who gives free rein to sin with no hope for anything beyond this life, to another who may become a model citizen who acknowledges that even a godless quasi-righteousness can exalt a nation; from the religionist who refuses to carry arms in times of war, to the genocidal maniac serving his concept of truth by stamping out God's "enemies;" from everyday people going about the business of everyday life, to committed Christians pursuing the will of God in ministry—all are shaped, to a greater or lesser degree, by their own ideas and beliefs regarding God and eternity. Without an accurate understanding of who God really is, humanity will serve false gods. And without an accurate understanding of God's character of love, human character goes into decline.

Christians are presumed to be generally gentle and kind…well, perhaps most of the time. But what about when a situation seems to call for gossip or destructive criticism or indifference to human woe or venting destructive emotions, or even sometimes taking human life? Do we not see God at times throughout history reacting in these same ways?

We need to understand that the human mind has an extraordinary capacity for kindness, yet in our selfish condition we often make exceptions for those we consider blameworthy, especially those "demonized" humans we imagine God must abhor. When we cause suffering for such people, we may convince ourselves that it's not really wrong. After all, we rationalize, doesn't God do similar things in His vengeance? Believing that God is the direct executor of the wages of sin subtly influences the human mind to think that, "In this case, I can do it too."

Historically the "church" has carried the traditional view of God as being a destroyer to its logical conclusion, sometimes by even burning to death their opponents.[22] Religious bigots have bloodied the pages of history with unspeakable crimes directly inspired by their biased picture of God.

Jesus predicted two thousand years ago that it would be this way. "[T]he time is coming that whoever kills you will think that he offers God service," He said. History confirms His prediction. How could we, as Christians, have been so blind, so callous, so indifferent to human life? Jesus distills the answer down to its core. "[T]hese things they will do to you," He continues, "because they have not known the Father nor Me." [23]

Contemplate the implications of that statement for a moment. Because Scripture gives so many examples of God's wiping out His enemies,

---

[22] Henry Charles Lea. *A History of the Inquisition of the Middle Ages.* (New York: Harper & Brothers, Franklin Square, 1867), I, 222-3.

[23] John 16:2, NKJV, emphasis supplied.

Christians have become confused regarding the interpretation of Jesus' words. They have concluded that when we destroy enemies, we're legitimately doing so as God's agents, but when they destroy us, they are fulfilling Jesus' prediction by persecuting us for doing what is right. We also generally view our enemy as God's enemy and like to imagine ourselves as His sword of justice.

For war to occur in the first place the soldiers involved must first be convinced their cause is righteous and their enemy's is evil. Yet is it possible that Jesus meant that wherever people kill each other, for whatever reason, neither side bears the approval of the true God of heaven? Jesus says they will do these things because they know neither Jesus nor His Father.

It takes little imagination to understand that traditional views of God as One who runs out of patience to the point where He resorts to deadly force, can only lead downward—where political power is viewed as a divine mandate to compel the conscience of the politically weak. In czarist Russia, as well as pre-revolutionary France, for example, the church's connection with and control over civil power led to terrifying abuses, resulting in an over-correction producing atheistic regimes. If this is Christianity, the people decided they wanted nothing to do with it. Communism itself began as a protest against religious cruelty.

The Holocaust is a modern case in point. A strong tradition of Judeo-Christian ethics didn't stop good, civilized people from supporting a regime which spilled the blood of millions in an attempt to exterminate an entire race perceived as undeserving of mercy. Where was the outrage? Where was the conviction that causing deaths on any scale was intrinsically wrong? The answer is fear, the underlying weapon used by evil to intimidate the reticent into silence and complicity, and the apostle John said, "[P]erfect love casts out fear."[24]

Northern Ireland, Bosnia, Kosovo, Iraq, Afganistan—all further illustrate the passion with which sectarian sides, believing they carry the flag of God for a righteous cause, killed and maimed innocent civilians and destroyed their own homeland in a seemingly endless bloodletting, presumably praying for the blessing of their fierce, nationalistic God before sallying forth on missions of destruction. There are no wars bloodier than religious wars, and efforts to bring stability to such regions

---

[24] 1 John 4:18, NKJV.

find religious fervor an almost impossible hurdle to overcome, politically generated peace accords notwithstanding.

If God can use force to get attention, then His followers should logically be allowed to rely on similar tactics to do His work. Civilization cannot rise any higher morally than their concept of Deity. "Ye are of your father . . . ," said Jesus, "and the works of your father ye will do."[25]

Without a settled conviction that hurting and destroying others is inherently wrong without exception, society positions itself over an ethical bottomless pit, with no protective absolutes to break its moral fall. Where shall we find a model for such settled conviction if we do not find it in God? Our view of God will always shape how we treat those around us. While both history and a surface reading of Scripture seem to represent God as a destroyer, the nagging questions prompt us to sense that there must be more to understand. Scripture predicts a time when "darkness shall cover the earth, and deep darkness the people."[26] Surely our world today is dark through misapprehension of God. We don't understand those moments when *agape* love seems to give way to unspeakable wrath and violence. And where is God when everything seems to go wrong in our life?

So come with me now on a journey through God's word, as we revisit the scenes of many ages-old, mysterious judgments of God. Let us push back the clouds of confusion that have enshrouded what appears to be His destructive side as we bring them into the light and we shall see that indeed, "God is light and in Him is no darkness at all."[27]

In the days of Christ those who opposed Him displayed the spirit of intolerance and repeatedly sought to silence Him. That same spirit often lives today where new insights threaten long-established views. Some will bitterly condemn anything that disturbs or threatens to undermine long-held preconceived ideas and traditions. But those with open minds and longing hearts who persevere, who are willing to evaluate the consistency and Scriptural basis of this new perspective before allowing prejudice to close their mind will be rewarded. As others before them have done, they may find themselves receiving it with joy.

---

[25] John 8:44, KJV.

[26] Isaiah 60:2, NKJV

[27] 1 John 1:5, NKJV.

2

God's Perfect Portrait

*"God is light, and in Him
is no darkness at all." (1John 1:5, KJV)*

You say God doesn't have a dark side? Really? What about Noah's
flood? What about Sodom and Gomorrah? What about eternally
burning hell? Drowning humans? Burning them alive? Burning them alive
forever? Some would say this picture of God is very dark. God seems to
be saying, "Obey me or I'll burn you—forever"? Doesn't this contradict
everything that God claims to be—merciful and gracious, patient, and
abounding in goodness and truth—including His commitment to free will?
Does this not throw the entire subject into confusion?

The God of Freedom
God's immense respect for our freedom, little discussed in religion, is
nonetheless paramount to understanding and appreciating the truth about
His character. Throughout these pages you will read much about freedom—our freedom to choose His ways or ours; our freedom to turn
away from Him, to spurn His love and demand that He exit our
personal space. This may at first seem strange given how many view God's
sovereignty as this: He always gets His way no matter what. But it is
inextricably tied to love, for without each person having freedom to reject
God without fear, it would be impossible to love Him from true
appreciation for that true character.

This is where we part ways with most of the religions of the world.
Insisting that God fiercely protects the freedom of even His worst enemies
is scandalous and blasphemous to many people. But this is because they

have no appreciation for true freedom or consider the central role it plays in providing us capacity to return His love.

God's love first led Him freely to give us His Son to provide a ransom for us when we were lost and dead in trespasses and sins and there was no other hope for us. But more relevant to the present topic, God also provided Him for a role model of His and His Father's character in order that we might pattern our characters after His own. Jesus said, "If you had known Me, you would have known My Father also. "[1]

God, As Jesus Revealed Him

Jesus revealed a creative, redemptive, healing God, who never brought needless pain to a sensitive soul. Even when in love He rebuked the leaders of His day, we can almost hear the tears in His voice as He uttered His scathing words, which rather than being destructive, were designed to redeem.

Startled by His disciples' suggestion that He call down fire upon the Samaritans who had slighted Him, He responded, "You do not know what kind of spirit you are of."[2] What does this tell us about God the Father? Would the fact that God performed such an act alter its "spirit"? Or is the evil nature of such an act eternally carved in granite? This event in our Lord's life suggests the latter. Burning humans alive in the name of religion is always and only the work of an evil spirit; Jesus insists it is not something our loving heavenly Father would do.

Jesus healed the ear of Malchus, the high priest's servant, gently rebuking Peter who had severed it while trying to cut off his head, saying, "Put your sword in its place; for all who take the sword will perish by the sword."[3] "Love your enemies," He said. "[B]less those who curse you, do good to those who hate you, and pray for those who spitefully use you and persecute you."[4] Why? *"That you may be sons of your Father in heaven."*[5]

---

[1] John 8:19, NKJV.

[2] Luke 9:55, NASV.

[3] Matthew 26:52, NKJV; Revelation 13:10.

[4] Matthew 5:44, NKJV.

[5] Matthew 5:45, NKJV, emphasis supplied.

God the Father as Jesus consistently presents Him, does not behave toward His enemies as other portions of Scripture seem to say. In the face of such apparent contradictions, we hear God saying, "My child, you must go deeper in the word."

The Man, Christ Jesus

Jesus was a man's man who walked great distances on the dusty roads of ancient Palestine, traveling stretches for which people today are awarded prizes. He taught vast multitudes, healing the sick, rebuking demons, standing his ground fearlessly before authority figures, telling them things they didn't want to hear, rising early while others slept to spend time with His Father. If ever one were qualified to take command of armies, it was He. Yet He refused the sword of earthly conquest held out to Him and chose instead the path to Calvary.

An Eye For An Eye?

"You have heard that it was said, 'An eye for an eye and a tooth for a tooth,'" but Jesus said. "I tell you not to resist an evil person. But whoever slaps you on your right cheek, turn the other to him also. If anyone wants to sue you and take away your tunic, let him have your cloak also. And whoever compels you to go one mile, go with him two. Give to him who asks you, and from him who wants to borrow from you do not turn away."[6] Today people of depth and moral substance ponder this Man with wonder. From where did He acquire His intimate familiarity with the fine points of greatness? He carried the word of God built into His inner life. "He who is slow to anger is better than the mighty, And he who rules his spirit than he who takes a city."[7] Jesus—so sound as a human, so full of insight and peace and power—never descended to self-serving in His daily human interactions. He rose above those common instincts and, in benevolence and warmth toward all, always continued to do right.

Some have suggested that Jesus came the first time to show the kindly side of God, but when He returns in glory He will then demonstrate His vengeance. However, nothing in the gospel record supports that view which rests on a human version of justice that is very different from how the Bible defines it. Scripture says Jesus is the same "yesterday, today and

---

[6]Matthew 5:38-42, NKJV.

[7] Proverbs 16:32, NKJV.

forever" and that He doesn't change.[8] God cannot and will not require humans to adhere to a standard He rejects for Himself. His commandments form not only the foundation of His government in heaven and on earth; they actually depict His character in words[9] as a novelist draws the inner life of characters with the pen. The principle which says "You shall not kill," which Jesus expanded to mean You shall not hate or damage in any way, originates in the heart of His Father God.

Reviewing the life of our Lord from Bethlehem to the Mount of Olives, from which He ascended to return to heaven, we find no evidence of any inclination to force on others allegiance to Himself, little we could interpret as destructive. "[T]he Son of Man did not come to destroy men's lives, but to save them."[10] In fact, there was nothing in His life to correspond to a presumed destructive side of God. Yet the life of Jesus offers insights into God's ultimate plans for dealing with the terrible problem of sin.

Far more relevant than we have realized was a behavior of His, little commented on up to now. When spurned or subjected to disrespect, when He conversely longed for fellowship and the opportunity to teach, He deferred to those who rejected Him and simply walked away. He accepted that His "grace in the face of rejection will be a witness to them"[11] and kindly left the place where He was not wanted.

The God Who Goes Away

Throughout Jesus life there were occasions when He longed to bless and benefit the people, but they didn't want His blessings. Too shallow to understand the depth of His love, they often turned Him away. What did Jesus do at such times? Was He wrathful? Did His white hot anger flash out to teach them a lesson? Remember, He had access to power to respond in any way He wanted—yes, with anger and violence if He chose. But what did He do when people rejected Him? His little-noticed response contains great lessons for us today, because in everything He did He revealed the Father.

---

[8] Hebrews 13:8, NKJV; Malachi 3:6; James 1:17.

[9] See Psalm 119: 172; Jeremiah 23:6; 33:16. [10]

Luke 9:56, NKJV.

[11] Mark 6:11, TR.

25

The Crisis in Nazareth

The first time we're told of was in Nazareth, His home town. According to Luke, after His baptism the Holy Spirit guided Him into the wilderness of temptation. Returning from that experience to where He was best known, He entered Nazareth where He was raised. His fame spread "through all the surrounding district." He enjoyed the praises of all as He taught in their synagogues.[12] "[A]s was His custom, He entered the synagogue on the Sabbath, and stood up to read,"[13] says Scripture. Everything went well for awhile.

But something He said filled them with sudden rage. When He referred to the many times the Lord favored the gentiles over the Jews, they ignored the fact that often the Jews did not want His blessings. Their national prejudice was ignited at the reminder of God's favoring the very ones whom they despised, so much so that they "drove Him out of the city, and led Him to the brow of the hill . . . in order to throw Him down the cliff."[14]

Do you think He wanted to leave His family and friends, those who had nurtured and encouraged Him throughout His growing years? Did He not have other things to share with them, rich layers of grace and truth to impart? Yet Scripture says, "[P]assing through their midst, He went His way," came to Capernaum, and settled there. So angry were they at His giving recognition to gentiles that they wanted to murder Him, so he moved to another city to preserve His life.[15]

He didn't want to leave, but He left anyway, because He always obeyed the guidance of God's Spirit in His life. And in everything He did He reflected the Father.

The Madmen of Gadara

Another event in the life of Jesus occurred following a wind-swept crossing of the Sea of Galilee. When they arrived on the shores of Gadara, one or two demon-possessed madmen[16] burst out of the tombs and rushed them. The disciples instantly scattered in every direction. But not Jesus. He calmly stayed, and when the disciples finally returned they discovered

---

[12] Luke 4:15, NAS.
[13] Luke 4:16, NAS.
[14] Luke 4:29, NAS.

[15] Luke 4:31, 32, NAS; Matthew 4:13-16, NAS.

[16] Matthew says two, but Mark says one.

26

the former madmen sitting quietly, clothed, and in their right mind. Jesus had healed them. This profoundly affected the surrounding populous, who alternated between fear and awe as they considered what had just happened to these men.

However, one event occurred in connection with their deliverance that provoked great feelings of resentment related to this healing. The demons had requested to be allowed to enter a herd of swine feeding nearby and Jesus allowed it, whereupon the swine, about two thousand in number, rushed down the steep embankment and drowned in the sea.

The herdsmen were filled with consternation and the owners were most likely livid. Perhaps care for the swine included financial responsibility as well; we're not told. But we do know that the herdsmen ran into the city reporting on what had just happened and brought everyone back with them.

"And behold, the whole city came out to meet Jesus; and when they saw Him, they implored Him to leave their region."[17] Jesus didn't want to leave; He had come to this place for a reason. Was it that He had things to teach them, things they needed to know? Did He want to rest from the unceasing labor that constantly wore on Him? We can only surmise. Nevertheless, "[g]etting into a boat, Jesus crossed over the sea"[18] and returned to the place from which He had just come.

We seldom think of other options Jesus had at such times. Why didn't He rise up in protest, telling the populous that they had no business herding swine anyway, and putting the people in their place? Wasn't eating swine's flesh forbidden by Leviticus 11:7? He could have gotten into a theological debate over what they were presumably doing and left His opponents in emotional shambles. But no. He didn't argue. He didn't raise His voice. With His disciples He simply got into the boat He had come in and returned back across the sea. In this action we do well to remember that He depicted not only His own character but that of His Father as well. "He will not shout, nor raise his voice, nor cause it to be heard in the street."[19]

---

[17] Matthew 8:34, NAS.

[18] Matthew 9:1, NAS.

[19] Isaiah 42:2 WEB.

Samaritan Rejection

Only Jesus knew that this would be His last trip to Jerusalem. On this journey He sent some messengers before the main company to find suitable lodging and to make other appropriate arrangements for their stay. The messengers went ahead into a city of Samaria, maybe even where Jesus had once met a woman at a well, and at her word the entire community had come out to hear Him speak. At that time they had believed Him to be the Messiah and received Him as such. Maybe He anticipated other similar speaking opportunities this time. One may imagine that the messengers didn't expect to encounter trouble in Samaria.

But Jesus' ultimate destination was Jerusalem. Upon learning of this, the animosity existing between Samaria and Jerusalem, dating back to the days of Nehemiah, ignited the resentment of the Samaritans. It was common for the people of these cities to want nothing to do with each other, certainly not to offer lodging to individuals passing through on their way to the other city. So the messengers were flatly denied the expected hospitality for Jesus and His disciples.

Notice Jesus' response to this direct insult. When James and John informed Him of their rudeness, they concluded with an offer posed as a question. "[D]o you want us to command fire to come down from heaven and consume them?"[20]

This outcome was what they had expected and they were eager to utilize the supernatural powers Jesus had given them previously on their missionary ventures to carry out what they believed was God's will against His enemies. Yet if you have come to know Jesus well, you can imagine the pained look that must have come over His face. No. We won't be doing anything of the sort. He did not, would not, respond in such a way. When faced with prejudice and rejection of a humble request for a simple kindness, He did not reflect the same spirit back to them. He may have hoped for one last chance to teach the people, and everything in Him may have longed to visit where He had before been received with such love. Yet Scripture says He merely moved on to another village. No wrath, resentment, or indignation here as might have been our response. He never forced His way in anywhere. Always He met rejection with the greatest

---

[20] Luke 9:54, NASV.

28

courtesy. What can we learn of the Father's character in these stories of Jesus' kind response to rejection? He merely, reluctantly, withdrew and went somewhere else.

Yes, there are times and situations in which God walks away. But it is *always* based on human choice and initiative.

Jesus Demonstrates the Anger of God

"He entered again into the synagogue, and there was a man there who had his hand withered. They watched him, whether he would heal him on the Sabbath day, that they might accuse him. He said to the man who had his hand withered, 'Stand up.' He said to them, 'Is it lawful on the Sabbath day to do good, or to do harm? To save a life, or to kill?' But they were silent. When he had looked around at them with *anger,* being *grieved at the hardening of their hearts*, he said to the man, 'Stretch out your hand.' He stretched it out, and his hand was restored as healthy as the other. The Pharisees went out, and immediately conspired with the Herodians against him, how they might destroy him."[21]

When we consider how Jesus related to feelings of anger, we can see here how He modeled the way we should respond. When we look for examples of when Jesus might have gotten angry, we usually think of the times He cleared the temple, or possibly the time He cursed a fig tree. However, in none of these accounts is it recorded that He got angry. John says, "[H]e made a scourge [whip] of cords, and drove them all out of the temple, with the sheep and the oxen; and He poured out the coins of the money changers and overturned their tables"[22] Although we might envision Him exploding with rage on those occasions, Scripture doesn't report anything about anger during those events.

However, as the above text says, just before He healed a man's withered hand He looked around Him *angrily*. This provides an important clue that an examination of this event in Christ's life promises key insights on how He dealt with His own anger, both here and possibly at other times. Since the antithesis of anger is arguably joy, let us first take a closer look at joy to discover key insights about anger.

Studies of the human brain and how we experience emotions have led brain scientists to identify six major negative emotions people experience

---

[21] Mark 3:1-6, WEB, emphasis supplied.

[22] 2:15, NAS.

29

that can cause problems if one does not learn how to properly relate to and recover from them. The normal brain, according to these studies, is designed to reside in a condition they call 'joy.' This joy is not 'happiness' as we usually define it but rather the joy of being bonded with another mind and heart, particularly with someone who is glad to be with us.[23]

This joy is not just an occasional emotion we might experience sporadically, but rather it involves living with a sense of knowing that someone genuinely wants to be with us. This is now known from studies to be the most basic and intense craving of the human brain. This desire for joy lies at the deepest levels of human subconsciousness and involves the bonding circuits that deeply connect us with another person.

So what does this have to do with anger and Jesus? It has a great deal to do with it, for living a life continually resting in the mindset of joy means you never lose sight of your true identity and thus can remember how to act like yourself no matter what other kind of emotion you may find yourself experiencing. Having someone who knows you well and loves you unconditionally provides a stability and perspective with an emotional anchor so that you can avoid acting out of character while experiencing the intensity of some negative emotion.

Because Jesus lived every moment of His human life on earth in constant fellowship with His Father, and because He anchored Himself securely in His Father's love every morning, He modeled for us how we may avoid becoming overwhelmed by any negative emotion or experience that we may encounter. Jesus demonstrated how to act like our true selves no matter what circumstance we may experience. Therefore, by studying how Jesus acted in all kinds of situations and emotions, we can learn much about being faithful to our true identity while we experience negative emotions just as He experienced them.

Interestingly, the story in Mark 3:1-6 is the only one in Scripture specifically mentioning Jesus becoming angry. Thus this story serves as the model for us whenever we have to deal with the emotion of anger. Keep in mind that Jesus endured constant harassment and hounding, facing what we might call 'sting operations' intended to trap Him, discredit His ministry, and diminish His effectiveness. Jealous religious leaders felt threatened by Jesus' popularity and incensed over His teachings and

---

[23] James G. Friesen, Ph.D. et. al. *The Life Model: Living From the Heart Jesus Gave You.* (East Peoria, IL: Shepherd's.House, Inc., 2004), pp. 61-68.

example, partly because He presented a loving God in sharp contrast with their dark teachings about Him. If this God of whom Jesus spoke came to be accepted by the world, the leaders saw that the common people would soon rebel against their corrupt system of power and control. The end result would be that the entire social structure might collapse if people took Jesus too seriously. The leaders were therefore becoming desperate to put an end to the growing, undermining influence of Jesus' teachings.

Jesus realized as He walked into the synagogue that this was another setup intended to discredit Him concerning the keeping of the Sabbath. The Jews (not God) had classified healing as an act of working, and since work was forbidden by God at any time on the Sabbath day, if they could catch Him healing someone on the Sabbath they could then publicly declare Him to be a lawbreaker and invalidate His claims to represent God with any authority. They also knew Jesus well enough to trust that His intense compassion would not allow Him to ignore a man with a withered hand; therefore, they had arranged the whole setup with this purpose in mind.

Because Jesus always kept open His connection with His Father through the Spirit, He was not intimidated by this trap. "He looked around at them with anger, being grieved at the hardening of their hearts." Here we see that Jesus experienced an anger rooted in grief that the leaders' hearts were hardening as their opportunity for eternal life was slipping away. The connection He had with His Father prevented His anger from being about Himself, rooted in personal offense or self-centeredness. He did as the apostle Paul admonished, "Be angry, and yet do not sin,"[24] for feelings of anger are not sin when they are born of genuine righteous indignation aroused in defense of the Father's honor, so long as we also reflect the humble, caring Spirit of the Father. These are the kinds of things Jesus felt as He "looked around at them with anger."

A Key Question

At this point in the story we need to ask a key question. What would Jesus do if He had not been angry? What would He have done with any intense negative emotion like shame, fear, anger, or any other? How would He have acted out of His true identity had He not been feeling any negative emotion?

---

[24] Ephesians 4:26, NAS.

Could there be any other reasonable answer than that, if Jesus were not angry He most likely would heal this man's withered hand, Sabbath or no? So did Jesus act any differently while experiencing intense emotion than He would were He feeling normal? The answer is clear —He would have acted exactly the same with or without the negative emotion.

We can apply this important principle to any other event in Jesus' life in order to understand better why He acted the way He did under various circumstances. If Jesus had felt anger while cleansing the temple, would He have done any differently than if He had not been angry? The right thing to do is to always act out our true self, our true identity given us by God. Jesus' example educates us as to how we may respond in any situation and any emotion instead of forgetting who we are and acting out the natural instincts of our heart, the grievous character of the enemy, only to regret it later.

Remember that His Father through the Holy Spirit was the most significant Person in His life, always there, never surprised by the traps and setups with which Jesus constantly dealt. His Father's hand kept Him steady as He journeyed through life eventually to end at the cross. Negative emotions sometimes assailed Him, but sharing His Father's heart, He passed successfully through every challenge. In the way He related to anger He modeled how we may respond when we struggle with dark feelings. No matter how He felt, He did the right thing—the thing He had begun to do before the dark feelings came.

This then is how God deals with anger when He experiences those feelings in His heart. We have seen Jesus angry. What did He do? He kept on doing the right thing for the healing of His people. Terribly hurt or grieved, He nevertheless didn't change His purposes but rose above His feelings to accomplish the good He had planned. Visions of God brutalizing His children for any reason exist only in society's imagination.

Jesus Saves—and Heals

The original word translated "save" or "saved" is also many times translated into the word *healed*; these two words mean the same thing. Because many do not realize this, they imagine that "being saved" means going to heaven. But this is only a small part of what God wants to do in our lives. His intention is to save us back to our original design to be reflectors of His great heart of love, living in such close intimacy with Him that everything we think, feel, and act out will reflect how He thinks, feels and acts. Thus He saves humans through oneness with Himself, through a deepening relationship of trust with Him. Our good works merely reveal that this union of intimacy exists. Through this relationship He transforms our thinking[25] and thus our disposition from what the world and our own sinful nature have taught us about our perceptions of reality and truth, enabling us to think and live in the totally different heavenly way, thus fitting our characters to enjoy eternal life with Him in His kingdom of love.

The Atonement

This model is God's ideal for us; He calls it the Atonement, or At-one-ment, the restoration of humans back into oneness with Himself. But what does this really mean? It is not what so many have come to assume about this word, that it is appeasing the anger of an offended God who contrived a way to have His own Son killed in order to make a way to forgive repentant sinners. Far from this dark picture of God, the truth about healing atonement or restoration through intimacy with His people, this at-one-ment, is actually found most clearly in our human experience through the example of a healthy marriage. Let's let Jesus explain.

The Pharisees came to test him and asked, "Is it lawful for a man to divorce his wife?" He answered, "What did Moses command you?" They said, "Moses allowed a certificate of divorce to be written, and to divorce her." But Jesus said to them, "For your hardness of heart, he wrote you this commandment. But from the beginning of the creation, God made them male and female. For this cause a man will leave his father and mother, and will join to his wife, and the two will become one flesh, so that they are no longer two, but one flesh. What therefore God has joined together, let no man separate."[26]

The religious leaders in Jesus' day attempted to be meticulous law-keepers. They believed that God was only interested in works, performance, outward behavior while completely ignoring their disposition, spirit, and attitudes toward those around them. Focusing only on the external and imagining that heavenly living had little to do with the

---

[25] Romans 12:2; 2 Corinthians 3:18.

[26] Mark 10:2-9 WEB.

content of their heart, their relationships with other people reflected this, and their marriages suffered as a result. Because they saw Jesus' teachings and ideas about God as threatening their stiff, demanding, legal version of Him, they decided to challenge Jesus with a legal question about divorce. Thus they thought to discredit Him in front of the people by showing that He disrespected the laws of Moses which defined what it meant to be an obedient follower of God and a good Jew.

Sadly what they failed to recognize was that their external-only religion was worthless compared to what Jesus wanted to give them. Jesus came to this earth to reveal the immense love of a gentle, compassionate Father, not a demanding One, waiting to punish every infraction of His strict demands, as religion tends to portray Him. The God Jesus came to reveal was far more interested in cultivating relationships than in studying performance. The answer Jesus gave in this exchange about divorce reveals God's desire to have His children grow up to become capable of entering into such an intimacy with Him that they can become a bride for His Son. He wants children who understand Him and can enjoy all the love and respect and joy that is possible in a relationship like that of a close marriage bond.

The religious leaders had in mind a completely different paradigm for a correct relationship to God. Jesus revealed to them their actual problem. It was not whether divorce could be considered legal in the eyes of God. It was the hardness of their own heart that led them to want a divorce from their wives in the first place. By referring these men back to the story of creation, Jesus pointed to the original design, which was starkly different from what these religious men had imagined God had in mind. These leaders believed in a system of earning God's favor by trying to keep myriads of rules while ignoring the condition of their heart. Jesus was sent to this earth to announce that God's favor was already there, simply waiting for us to believe in it and embrace it.[27]

In the Garden of Eden
What do we find in the origins to which Jesus referred that can tell us what God had in mind for His original design and to what He intends to restore us if we will only let Him?   He said,   "Let us make man in our

---
[27] Luke 2:13-14; 4:18-19.

image, after our likeness...." "God created man in his own image. In God's image he created him; male and female he created them."[28]

This is what Jesus quoted in answer to the men who were looking for excuses to divorce their wives in order to acquire one more to their liking. God's original design as created was two uniquely complementary human beings reflecting His own heart of love that had the potential and natural desire to draw closer to each other in intimacy until it could be said that they were no longer two but one. Jesus explains this in order that we might grasp God's purpose for our existence as well as for marriage. But more importantly by far, He portrayed marriage as an active parable revealing to us the far greater purpose God has for us. God intended for humanity to ultimately enter into something like a "marriage" experience with Deity to the point that they could be His bride in a state of At-one-ment. "For this cause a man will leave his father and mother, and will join to his wife, and the two will become one flesh, so that they are no longer two, but one flesh."[29]

If this sounds strange or almost scandalous, consider that Paul picks up on this same theme in Ephesians when discussing relationships between husbands and wives, a passage also largely misunderstood, again because our own hearts are still hard today. After trying to explain how husbands and wives should interact, respect, and love each other mutually, he concludes his discussion by doing what Jesus did—referring us back to God's original design at creation.

"Even so husbands also ought to love their own wives as their own bodies. He who loves his own wife loves himself. For no man ever hated his own flesh; but nourishes and cherishes it, even as the Lord also does the assembly; because we are members of his body, of his flesh and bones. For this cause a man will leave his father and mother, and will be joined to his wife. The two will become one flesh. This mystery is great, but I speak concerning Christ and of the assembly."[30]

"In Him"

A vital component of this heavenly marriage and God's design to heal us and bring us back to His original plan involves the theme "in Him" or "in

---

[28] Genesis 1:26-27 WEB.

[29] Mark 10: 7, 8, WEB.

[30] Ephesians 5:28-32 WEB.

Christ." He says it is a "mystery" which He presents in symbols in a tireless effort to engage our minds and trigger our understanding. Sadly, in most churches today this theme is scarcely noticed and rarely mentioned, even though Scripture presents it as a prominent Biblical topic. Whereas this theme should be number one and studied by all, it hardly registers a blip on the churches' radar.

Jesus said, "I am the living bread that came down out of heaven; if anyone eats of this bread, he will live forever; and the bread also which I will give for the life of the world is my flesh."[31] Here He equates His flesh with bread, yet *living* bread. What do we do with bread? We eat it and it nourishes us, literally becoming our own body. That's the purpose for bread. Clearly in these words He must mean that we are to symbolically "eat" His flesh; but living bread is alive, sentient. This bread that our Lord offers us has consciousness; it is a Person. How do we eat a conscious Being in order to complete the marriage metaphor? How can He literally become a part of us, acquire a place deep within us?

"He who eats my flesh and drinks My blood abides in Me, and I in him."[32] Eat His flesh? Drink His blood? We cannot imagine it! Jesus soon made clear[33] that His flesh and blood symbolize *His words*. Yet, still, what powerful imagery to explain returning to God's original design and making us eligible to live forever. The experience He describes will make us immortal beings! As ingested food goes into the body to sustain and empower it, so too does His word ingested into the mind create the reality of mutual abiding.

Just before leaving our world to return to the Father, this marriage relationship was uppermost in His mind. He said, "Abide in Me and I in you. As the branch cannot bear fruit of itself unless it abides in the vine, so neither can you unless you abide in Me. . . . abide in My love."[34]

God assures us that each of us may have this close, intimate relationship with Deity; by studying His character His ways become reproduced in us. His word also heals us and brings us back to our original design to be reflectors of the truth about our loving Father.

---

[31]John 6:51, NAS.

[32]John 6:56, NAS.

[33] v. 63, NAS.

[34] John 15:1-11, NAS

Still other Scriptural metaphors clearly symbolize this intimate relationship. Jesus told a story about a wedding to which one guest arrived without a wedding garment. "Friend," said the host (representing the Father), how did you come in here without wedding clothes?"[35] The host had provided a festive garment for every guest, and to come to the wedding without it would be strange and unthinkable. That garment is alive, sentient, aware and saturated in love. And as the host, God the Father, places it over our shoulders, it actually soaks in all through us as it transforms us on the inside. This is the presence of the Holy Spirit which, if our eyes could be opened to spiritual realities, we could see actually living inside us. The marriage is complete. This symbol, found throughout Scripture, underscores the kind of intimacy which God longs to create with His people.

"Awake, awake. Clothe yourself in your strength, O Zion; Clothe yourself in your beautiful garments, O Jerusalem, the holy city."[36] Everywhere you look in Scripture, God admonishes us to put on our beautiful garments. The True Witness counseled the Laodicean church that white garments represents one of her most vital needs. "I advise you to buy from Me . . . white garments so that you may cloth yourself, and that the shame of your nakedness will not be revealed."[37] "He has clothed me with garments of salvation, He has wrapped me with a robe of righteousness, as a bridegroom decks himself with a garland, And as a bride adorns herself with her jewels."[38]

(Of course, not all references to garments translate into what we are talking about here. But they often do. It is a prominent theme throughout Scripture, sometimes symbolized as a "hedge" or a "shield.")

Notice the last reference that mentions obtaining "righteousness" through having this garment. The wedding garment, in fact, represents Christ living in us through the Holy Spirit, which is God's design for us. Many give lip service to this idea but too few understand what it really means by experience. Only the Holy Spirit has righteousness to give, to share; the only righteousness available to us in earth and sea and sky, the kind of righteousness which prepares us for heaven. Do you see that if we

---

[35] Matthew 22:12, NAS.

[36] Isaiah 52:1, NAS.

[37] Revelation 3:18, NAS.

[38] Isaiah 61:10, NAS.

want to enjoy heaven we must arrive there with the Holy Spirit living in our hearts? This is God's original design to which He is calling us back.

In this connection, have you noticed how often Scripture speaks of living "in Him"? You can almost open the Bible to any random page and find the author speaking of dwelling "in Christ." "To the praise of the glory of his grace, which He freely bestowed on us *in the beloved*."[39]

God can bestow His grace on us while we live "in Him." Why would we not live in Him every moment, sensitive to His abiding presence? "For in him we live, and move, and have our being."[40] "He made Him who knew no sin to be sin on our behalf, so that we might become the righteousness of God *in Him*."[41]

Immediately before His crucifixion and return to heaven, Jesus wanted to leave a treasured Gift for the blessing of those He would leave behind. "Do not let your heart be troubled," He comforted them. "[B]elieve in God, believe also in Me. In My Father's house are many dwelling places; if it were not so, I would have told you."[42] "If you love me, you will keep My commandments. I will ask the Father, and He will give you another Helper, that He may be with you forever; that is the Spirit of truth, whom the world cannot receive, because it does not see Him or know Him, but you know Him because He abides with you and will be in you."[43] Notice, the last thing He did before leaving this earth was to promise the Holy Spirit to His disciples to be His representative to them and to us.

His Message Today

And what is His message to us today? "Behold, I stand at the door and knock; if anyone hears My voice and opens the door, I will come in to him and will dine with him, and he with Me."[44] Where is Jesus? He is standing outside the door, knocking for entry. He wants us to know Him as He knows us. He wants us to know His true character, how He relates to others and to be privy to His divine purposes. He wants to share an intimate, insider's relationship with us.

---

[39] Ephesians 1:6, NAS, emphasis supplied..

[40] Acts 17:28, KJV.

[41] 2 Corinthians 5:21, NAS, emphasis supplied.

[42] John 14:1, NAS.

[43] John 14: 15-17, NAS.

[44] Revelation 3:20, NAS.

This is the ultimate reason for existing as a human being, to enter into this stunning, privileged relationship of being so intimate with God that we become no longer separate as two entities but one flesh with Him. This is the true meaning of at-one-ment. This is why Jesus came in human flesh—in order that humans who live in that same flesh may become one flesh with God, just as a married man and woman can enjoy the ecstasy of a one-flesh experience with each other as their hearts are united in the kind of love God has toward them. Toward this end He constantly draws us and seeks to educate our thinking. Although His efforts have produced limited success through the centuries, He has never been without those who have responded to Him. And prophecy is clear that before His return He will finally have *a people* who have come to understand and who choose to enter into this level of intimacy with His heart, which has been His ideal from the beginning of creation.

The Role of Law

The Pharisees and Sadducees pushed Christ aside in their fixation on the law which could never heal them. The law is only provided to inform; it has no capacity to cleanse. The apostle James says that the law is like a mirror that can give us a true picture of our condition when we look into it,[45] but that is the limit of its power. The law is just a written outline of God's character in one dimension. We must look to Christ the living One to observe God's character lived out in everything it means to be human.

Cleansing, healing, saving us back to our original design—all these are outside the scope of the law's ability and purpose. These require the involvement of two—the human and the divine, us and the tangible living Christ who comes close to us, revealing His great compassion for us and lifting us to Himself.

And then we remember. Yes, the law is just His character written down, not the real essence of who He is. It is His essence, the reality of Him, that we want.

But doesn't that law have a function in all this? Yes. The written law then becomes a barrier, a fence if you will, to warn us when we are tempted as well as to reveal the true condition of our selfish heart. Our part is to rest in the knowledge of the invisible presence of our Lord who

---

[45] 1:23.

then teaches us His paths.[46] The law will never heal or save us back to our original design. Only the power of the Holy Spirit can do that as He works quietly in the shadows of our mind to make Jesus a living reality in our day-to-day experience.

God intended that we abide in this intimate relationship with Deity. Thus it broke the heart of God when humanity went astray into the abyss of Godless selfishness and sin, because He knew the sorry end of that lifestyle. The human race was on a collision course with death—a death of their own making. Humanity would experience the consequences of living without the great Life Generator. Humanity would be hopeless, lost, and spiraling down a dark and lonely corridor ending in oblivion had not God intervened.

Who Delivered Christ to Die?

In the councils of heaven the plan was conceived for Christ to come to this dark earth and take all the results of sin upon Himself. He would shed His blood and die for the inhabitants of earth. Jesus was the Son of God sent to fulfill this mission and save us from our predicament of sin.[47] In the days leading up to the climax of this plan, near the end of His ministry, Jesus sought to prepare the minds of His disciples for the coming crisis. Repeatedly Christ tried to share the reality of His upcoming death with them. "For He taught His disciples and said to them, 'The Son of Man is being *delivered* into the hands of men, and they will kill Him.'" "Behold, we are going up to Jerusalem and the Son of Man will be *delivered* to the chief priests and to the scribes, and they will condemn Him to death."[48]

But a key question we must ask is this: Who was "delivering" Him? Judas certainly planned to, yet Jesus was not referring to him. Just who had the authority to deliver Jesus to death? The apostle Paul makes clear who "delivered" Him up:

"He that spared not his own Son, but *delivered Him up* for us all, how shall he not with him also freely give us all things?"[49] It was the Father who delivered Him (or released Him) to the destructive forces around Him.

---

[46] Psalm 25:4, NAS.

[47] Matthew. 1:21.

[48] Mark 9:31, NKJV, emphasis supplied. See also Matthew 26:2, 14, 15; 27:18; Mark 20:33, 34; 14:10; 15:1, 11; Luke 22:4; Acts 2:23.

[49] Romans 8:32, KJV.

Significantly, Pilate also "delivered" Christ over to be crucified, but not before our Lord informed the proud ruler he would have no power to do this if God did not allow it.[50]

Does this mean that the Father was complicit in the execution of His beloved Son? Not at all! At the cross "God was in Christ, reconciling the world to Himself,"[51] but the enormous heaviness of the darkness of our sins on Him caused Jesus to lose the sense of His Father's presence. According to their agreed-upon plan, conceived in the far reaches of eternity past, the Father could not lift His hand to help Him in any way, because Jesus was now experiencing the death of sinners. The Father and all the agencies of heaven stood down that day and "delivered up" our Savior to whatever fate awaited Him outside the circle of heavenly protection that surrounded Him. Jesus attested to this reality when on the cross He cried out the first line of a prophetic psalm He had no doubt memorized long before, "My God, My God, why have You forsaken Me?"[52] Clearly, while God's role in the crucifixion of His Son, the Sin-bearer, was to withdraw divine protection and release him to the powers of darkness,[53] with this one exception, God the Father had *no involvement* in the execution itself . . .

even though Scripture says He did!

> *'Awake, O sword, against My Shepherd, [a]gainst the Man who is My Companion,' [s]ays the Lord of hosts. 'Strike the Shepherd, [a]nd the sheep will be scattered.'*[54]

Jesus claims these words as a prophecy of Himself: "Then Jesus said to them [His disciples], 'All of you will be made to stumble because of Me this night, for it is written: "I will strike the Shepherd, [a]nd the sheep of the flock will be scattered."'"[55] Both Father and Son agree; God the Father

---

[50] John 19:10, 11.

[51] 2 Corinthians 5:19, NKJV.

[52] Matthew 27:46, NAS; Psalm 22:1, NAS.

[53] Even though He was released, those to whom He was released were still accountable for what they did when He was handed over to them.

[54] Zechariah 13:7, NKJV.

[55] Matthew 26:31, NKJV; Mark 14:27, NKJV.

claims to "strike" Christ, although we would certainly not describe it that way. The Old Testament prophecy from which He quotes also suggests use of a "sword," or violence, "Against the Man who is My Companion," a clear reference to the intimacy of relationship between Father and Son. Yes, Christ died violently, but not by His Father's hand. Isaiah 53, universally accepted within Christendom as a Messianic prophecy, says, "Surely he hath borne our griefs, and carried our sorrows: yet we did esteem him stricken, *smitten of God*, and afflicted." "Yet *it pleased the Lord to bruise him; he has put him to grief.*"[56]

Do we consider God's removal of His protection from humans as an act of aggression against them? Scripture insists that God "struck" His Son, yet is this how God strikes? Closer examination of Scripture reveals that God's wrath is expressed by His withdrawing and releasing humans to the destructive forces around them. Once understood, this pattern helps make sense of many other situations. But if this is true, why would God allow Himself to be described as the agent of execution?

Jerusalem Destroyed

In searching through Christ's life for clues about God's role in the final death of lost sinners, we find one incident particularly enlightening. For centuries God had sent prophets to Israel to warn them of the consequences of their entrenched rebellion against heaven and to plead with them to repent. At last He sent His Son.

But as Christ sat upon a colt on Mount Olivet's brow one of the last evenings before His death He looked out over the beautiful city of Jerusalem and wept, because He knew the people would shortly seal their centuries-long rejection of heaven through His own crucifixion. He saw the armies of Titus besiege the city some forty years in the future, saw indescribable woe descend upon the people, saw the temple of God in flames unquenchable through any human effort.

He also saw the interplay of invisible forces that would finally open the door to this catastrophe, and He wept. His thoughts found expression soon in a confrontation with the nation's religious leaders.

---

[56] Isaiah 53: 4, 10, NKJV, emphasis supplied.

.

"O Jerusalem, Jerusalem, the one who kills the prophets and stones those who are sent to her! How often I wanted to gather your children together, *as a hen gathers her chicks under her wings*, but you were not willing."[57]

Jerusalem perished after they, by crucifying the One sent to save them, abandoned their connection with God and thus their only life and protection. The symbol of a protecting parent bird, usually an eagle, spreading wings over its young, abounds in Scripture, revealing the nature of the relationship God wants to have with His people and their need of total dependence upon the heavenly provision available only in that connection. It was perhaps the nearest heaven could come to describing invisible realities in human language. Yet it was by no means the only symbol Scripture used to represent this same truth.

---

[57] Matthew 23:37, NKJV, emphasis supplied

3

How the
Bible Explains Itself

"For precept must be upon
precept, . . . line upon line, . . . here
a little, and there a little."
(Isaiah 28:10, KJV)

Imagine, if you will, that you live in a land where the word "tooth" means "tree stump." If you journey to my world and attempt to get your tree stump uprooted, you might get some interesting looks when you ask, "May I use your tractor to uproot my tooth?" How much progress would you make with this project until you learn how to speak in the local tongue? Likewise, our difficulty in seeing the true Bible picture of God's character is often a language problem—a problem easily cleared up when some careful comparisons are made within Scripture.

In order to see God in His beautiful character and reasonable mind, you will be asked to learn a new language, the language of Scripture. Where do you go to learn it? Not to the Internet. Not to a linguist. Not to the clergy. You will find this new language within the pages of the ancient Scriptures themselves, as it defines its own terms. We have too often made the mistake of using Webster's dictionary to define Biblical terms, and that has often caused unnecessary confusion. Regardless of our native tongue, allowing Scripture to provide its own definitions will help to clear up many long-standing mysteries about God's character.

For instance, to lay a proper foundation for discussing specific incidents of God's vengeance we must first look at some idiosyncrasies of Scripture and how God expresses Himself. In so doing we may then delve into other related themes. These are not digressions, however, for all the issues of redemption intersect in the central truth about the character of God. Therefore touching on these related themes, besides addressing some peculiarities of Scripture, can also help to unravel some of the mystery of God's actual role in destructive acts attributed to Him.

Paradoxical Principles

First, it is often helpful to learn to think in reverse in order to more easily understand truths of the kingdom of God. No one can ever come to know God as He desires to be known, until they begin to think and live by God's "paradoxical" principles. Of the numerous instances throughout Scripture we shall examine only these few:

• He who loves his life will lose it, and he who hates his life in this world will keep it for eternal life.[1]

• [T]o everyone who has will be given; and from him who does not have, even what he has will be taken away from him.[2]

• God has chosen the foolish things of the world to put to shame the wise, and God has chosen the weak things of the world to put to shame the things which are mighty; and the base things of the world and the things which are despised God has chosen, and the things which are not, to bring to nothing the things that are.[3]

• [T]hrough death He…destroy[ed]…the devil.[4]

The abundance of these apparent paradoxes in Scripture says something about God's way of thinking that is vital to understanding the present topic. "My thoughts are not your thoughts, [n]or are your ways My ways, says the Lord."[5] Public opinion almost never reflects the mind of God. Therefore, we should not be surprised to discover we have misunderstood in the arena of God's "vengeance" as in so many others.

---

[1] John 12:25, NKJV.

[2] Luke 19:26, NKJV.

[3] 1 Corinthians 1:27, 28, NKJV.

[4] Hebrews 2:14, NKJV.

[5] Isaiah 55:8, 9, NKJV.

45

There is always the need to be careful when approaching new ideas, as any perspective can easily be carried to excess. Accept only what the Bible clearly supports relying most importantly on the view of God provided by Jesus Christ. The point is, we should not be surprised to find heavenly truths that are the very reverse of popular beliefs and teachings.

When we consider "divine retribution" as *Christ's life* expressed it, how can we avoid seeing that something is amiss. There was no "divine retribution" in His life. No vengeance; no getting even. Perhaps truth on this topic lies opposite of where we have always believed. Can we understand "the wrath of God" and God's "anger" in ways other than we have understood them in the past?

The first step in decoding this mystery is to examine some Biblical contradictions, starting with the one below.

Biblical Contradictions

A prominent argument in Christendom, the issue of how law (works/obedience) and grace (faith) apply to our salvation will help us here. Some say we are saved by grace through faith, basing their belief on such texts as:

> • [B]y grace you have been saved through faith, and that not of yourselves; it is the gift of God, *not of works*, lest anyone should boast.[6]

> • [A] man is not justified by the works of the law but by faith in Jesus Christ, even we have believed in Christ Jesus, that we might be *justified by faith* in Christ and not by the works of the law; for by the works of the law no flesh shall be justified.[7]

On the other side of the picture we have this:

> • And I saw the dead, small and great, standing before God, and the books were opened. And another book was opened, which is the Book of Life. And the dead were judged *according to their works*, by the things which were written in the books. The sea gave up the dead who were in it, and Death and Hades delivered up the dead who were in them. And they were judged, each one *according to his works*.[8]

---

[6] Ephesians 2:8, 9, NKJV, emphasis supplied.

[7] Galatians 2:16, NKJV, emphasis supplied.

[8] Revelation 20:12, 13, NKJV, emphasis supplied.

• [F]aith without works is dead....A man is justified *by works*, and not by faith only.[9]

So here we have a classic Scriptural contradiction, providing a basis for argument, alienation, and division within Christendom.

None of this need happen, if Christians determined to harmonize these apparent contradictions through serious Bible study, allowing Scripture to be its own interpreter, until a clear picture emerges of the truth of the matter.

Juxtaposing ideas sometimes helps to clarify; therefore, at this point we shall introduce a format that will become familiar as we move along:

How does God save humans?

One Perspective	Another Perspective
[B]y grace you have been saved through faith, and that not of yourselves; it is the gift of God, not of works, lest anyone should boast.[10]	[F]aith without works is dead ...A man is justified by works and not by faith alone.[11]

In this case we are fortunate to have a third set of data that explains the apparent contradiction:

Comment

For in Jesus Christ neither circumcision [works] availeth anything, nor uncircumcision [faith]; but *faith which worketh by love*.[12]

Galatians 5:6 defines saving faith as a faith which "works" through a special kind of other-centered love called *agape*. Therefore, the works which humans cannot generate in and of themselves, flow out of the life powered by genuine faith. When heaven looks at a life and sees the "beauty of holiness" expressed in reverence for God, sensitivity to others' needs and feelings, and the ability to rise above the harmful instincts of our human nature, they know Someone else lives there besides the human

---

[9] James 2:20, 24, NKJV, emphasis supplied.

[10] Ephesians 2:8, 9, NKJV.

[11] James 2:20,24, NKJV.

[12] Galatians 5:6, KJV, emphasis supplied.

47

and His are the works they see. Paul in Galatians 2:16, KJV, calls this "the faith of Jesus Christ" or we might say, Jesus living out His life in the believer. This faith works, and the faith that works is the faith that saves, heals, transforms, restores.

The writings of Paul the apostle are sometimes hard to understand principally because we have not understood this dynamic which forms the very core of his message.

The Love of God

Agape, the great love principle, is the mortar that holds together the temple of the Lord. *Agape* will always do what is in the best interest of those who put their simple trust in God; in fact, of everyone who will let Him. If all else fails, *agape* stands fast forever.

But the *agape* idea cannot fully convey the depths of the emotional side of God's love for His children. Think what love it took for the Father to allow His unique and dearly beloved Son to come to this dark earth to live and die for you and me. It took far more than a principle to motivate that depth of emotion. God *is* love. "Love" does not describe how He acts but what He is as a Person. The Father loves us with a love far above ours for our children or anything else we can understand. He loves us in a personal way. In fact, it would not be a stretch to speak of God's love as a consuming, passionate fire.[13] If you have any doubts of His love for you, read the book of Hosea or Song of Solomon, great messages of God's love for His children, in prose, in poem, and metaphor.

Love Enforces the Law

God's kingdom is very different in key aspects to our systems. Human laws require that humans create and then enforce their laws. God's law on the other hand simply reflects who He is and requires nothing but heavenly *agape* to provide enforcement. In other words, God's laws are self-enforcing. Because the citizens of God's kingdom "do by nature the things contained in the law,"[14] there is no friction in them with the law. God's presence in the human heart produces natural righteousness, yet it is also true that while abiding in Him and still retaining free will, humans need a sin detector or standard of behavior to inform their decision making

---

[13] Zephaniah 3:17; Revelation 1:12; John 3:16; 14:15-17, etc.

[14] Romans 2:14, WEB

and to gauge whether they are truly living in harmony with His ways; that is, whether they are true fruit-bearing branches of the living vine[15] or mere pretenders. Therefore, God wrote down His character for us and proclaimed it from Mount Sinai.

Thus the Ten Commandments inform us, even as the living Lord Our Righteousness enables us. He is the living law. If we would walk with Him and be drawn into intimacy with Him, we must allow Him to change us into His own likeness of character in order that our ways may become like His. We may daily walk in intimate fellowship with Him, learning how His ways as set out in that holy law, are actually beautiful and desirable. But it requires converted hearts to perceive this; therefore, our attitude toward His Ten Commandments reveals whether or not we have been "born again."[16] It can be seen then, that obedience to those ten principles is ultimately about both defining and protecting our relationship with God, not so much about being saved and going to heaven someday. Day by day we may abide in Him, and as we invite and consent for Him to. abide in us, "being saved" takes care of itself as His indwelling Spirit works to will and to do through us what brings pleasure to the Father.[17]

Those who choose to enter into this intimate relation with God sooner or later find that Sabbath observance, found at the very heart of God's law, actually symbolizes the reality of this experience in their lives. The Sabbath literally means "rest," and the greatest kind of rest is freedom from depending on our own works of righteousness to earn God's favor. Thus the Sabbath, according to Scripture, is the ultimate sign of re-creation, rest in the Lord, living by faith, and depending totally on the God of love to heal and save us.

"Moreover also I gave them my Sabbaths, to be a sign between me and them, that they might know that I am Yahweh who sanctifies them."[18] This outward sign is a signal to the watching universe that we are not the ones trying to change ourselves but rather it is the Spirit of God, the God who is love, living inside of us that is doing the work of transformation.

---

[15] John 15:1-8.

[16] Jesus says we will know the true Christian "by his fruits" (Matthew 7:20; Galatians 5:22, 23) The law of God serves as fruit checker, whereby Christians and their associates gauge the reality of the believer's oneness with Christ through the Holy Spirit. If the experience is real, the fruit will be there.

[17] Philippians 2:13.

[18] Ezekiel 20:12 WEB.

Resting from our own efforts to change our lives by relying completely on the transforming power of God living inside of us, changing our thinking, perceptions, and resultant actions in the process, is best illustrated in the rest we choose to enjoy each week as we also refrain from work to support ourselves financially and physically. This is the true rest of the Sabbath as described in Hebrews 4—not a mere outward refraining from work but protected time when we can give ourselves without distraction to enjoying intimacy with the One who is becoming the love of our life and the source of all our joy.

Biblical Contradictions

Some may wonder what all this has to do with the fate of the lost. A little reflection will reveal that if the way God saves humans is through union with Himself, then eternal loss is simply a natural consequence of failure to enter into that unity. The symptoms relied on to diagnose this condition are the outward actions and behaviors that expose the true condition of the heart. To avoid a tragic end, we need to experience union with God through the Spirit.

We have explored how God will heal us through intimacy with Him if we let Him, plus we have studied how to address Biblical contradictions. Realizing that God does not contradict Himself, we need to continue studying until we are better able to grasp the full Biblical picture all the texts convey. In seeking to know the mind of God, until we have logically and Scripturally resolved evidence in contrast to our personal views, we cannot be sure we have arrived at truth.

Following are just a few of the perplexing apparent contradictions which have puzzled students of Scripture for years. Examining them more carefully provides insight into the way God sometimes expresses Himself and reveals a principle we may use in understanding what appears to be the destructive ways of God:

Who sends a lying spirit?

One Perspective	Another Perspective
[T]he Lord said, "Who will persuade Ahab to go up that he may fall at Ramoth Gilead?" ... [A] spirit came forward and stood before the Lord and said ... "*I will go out and be a lying spiri*t in the mouth of all his prophets."[19]	[I]t is impossible for God to lie ... God ... cannot lie.[20]

God says in the left-hand quotation that He sent out a lying spirit, yet the quotation on the right says God cannot lie. Obviously, this appears to be a contradiction. What does it mean? We have no Scripture clarification on this point. Next question:

Who led David to number Israel?

One Perspective	Another Perspective
[T]he *anger* of the Lord was aroused against Israel, and *He moved David* ... to ... number Israel and Judah.[21]	Now *Satan* stood up against Israel and moved David to number Israel.[22]

Again, we have no explanation in the immediate passages. The surface reader usually concludes that after prompting David to do this, God turned around and punished him for it.[23] Did God have anything to do with causing David to do something that was against His will and then punishing him for it? What kind of God is He, and can we trust such a God to be fair? Maybe this is another conundrum we need to unpack to discover how Scripture can more effectively explain itself.

---

[19] 1 Kings 22:20, 22, NKJV, emphasis supplied.

[20] Hebrews 6:18; Titus 1:2, NKJV.

[21] 2 Samuel 24:1, NKJV, emphasis supplied.

[22] 1Chronicles 21:1, NKJV, emphasis supplied..

[23] 2 Thessalonians 2:11, NKJV.

Who deceives?

One Perspective	Another Perspective
If a prophet is deceived and speaks a word, *I, the Lord,* have deceived that prophet . . . .[24]	*[Satan]* shall shall go out to deceive the nations which are in the four quarters of the earth." *[The] devil* . . . deceived them.[25]

It appears that both God deceives and Satan deceives, if you go strictly by the apparent message of these two texts. Is this another of those apparently contradictory Bible texts that through the years has confirmed the atheist in his unbelief and bewildered a multitude of Christians?

Whose idea was it to spy out the Promised Land?

One Perspective	Another Perspective
And *the Lord* spoke to Moses, saying, "Send men to spy out the land of Canaan, which I am giving to the children of Israel."[26]	Moses said, "And everyone of you came near to me and said, 'Let *us* send men before us, and let them search out the land."[27]

Again, we have no clarifying comment. Next question . . .

Who killed Saul?

One Perspective	Another Perspective
So Saul died for his unfaithfulness which he had committed against the Lord, because he did not keep the word of the Lord, and also because he consulted a medium for guidance, [b]ut he did not inquire of the Lord; therefore, *He [God] killed him,* and turned the kingdom over to David, the son of Jesse.[28]	Saul said to his armorbearer, "Draw your sword, and thrust me through with it" ... But his armorbearer would not. ... Therefore, *Saul took a sword and fell on it. ... So Saul ... died.*[29]

---

[24] Ezekiel 14:9, NRSV.

[25] Revelation 20:7, 8, 10, KJV.

[26] Numbers 13:1, 2, NKJV, emphasis supplied. [27] Deuteronomy 1:22, NKJV, emphasis supplied.

[28] 1 Chronicles 10:13, 14, NKJV, emphasis supplied.

[29] 1 Chronicles 10:4, 6, NKJV, emphasis supplied.

Who hardened Pharaoh's heart?

One Perspective	Another Perspective
And *the Lord* said to Moses, "When you go back to Egypt, see that you do all those wonders before Pharaoh which I have put in your hand. But *I will harden his heart* so that he will not let the people go."[30]	But when Pharaoh saw that there was relief, *he hardened his heart* and did not heed them, as the Lord had said ... But *Pharaoh hardened his heart* at this time also; neither would he let the people go.[31]

Is God furious?

One Perspective	Another Perspective
I am full of the fury of the Lord.[32]	Fury is not in Me [says the Lord].[33]

Here God seems to take responsibility for activities that we might say He did not actually do. We find no clarifying Biblical comment. No "counterpoint" statements exist for the following puzzling assertions either:

• But the Spirit of the Lord departed from Saul, and an evil spirit *from the Lord* troubled him.[34]

• God will *send* them [the wicked] strong delusion.[35]

• Is it not from the mouth of the Most High that good and bad come?[36]

• I ... *[the Lord]* create calamity [evil].[37]

• When you have come into the land of Canaan...and *I* put the leprous plague in a house....[38]

---

[30] Exodus 4:21, NKJV, emphasis supplied.

[31] Exodus 8:15, 32, NKJV, emphasis supplied.

[32] Jeremiah 6:11, NKJV.

[33] Isaiah 27:4, NKJV.

[34] 1 Samuel 16:11, KJV, emphasis supplied.

[35] 2 Thessalonians 2:11, NKJV, emphasis supplied.

[36] Lamentations 3:38.

[37] Isaiah 45:7, NKJV, emphasis supplied.

[38] Leviticus 14:34, 35, NKJV, emphasis supplied. 53

Hint of a Solution

While these few examples highlight the problem, there are some that hint of a solution.

Who killed the firstborn of Egypt?

One Perspective	Another Perspective
God speaking: "For *I* will pass through the land of Egypt on that night, and will *strike* all the firstborn in the land of Egypt, both man and beast; against all the gods of Egypt *I will execute judgment: I am the Lord.*"[39]	For the Lord will pass through to strike the Egyptians: and when He sees the blood on the... doorposts, the Lord will pass over the door and not allow *the destroyer* to come into your houses to strike you.[40]

Clearly, two actors share the stage of the disaster in the above action, the Lord and another being called *the destroyer*. The people could not ignore the Lord's instruction without peril to their own well being. Could the Lord protect all from the destroyer? Indeed He could have; He had the power but not necessarily the authority. The people themselves had the option of handing their own fortunes over to the God/god of their own choosing, depending on whom they obeyed. Thus God was in no way responsible for the Egyptian deaths that occurred that night. We will go into this more in Chapters 4, 7 and 9.

Did the Father play a role in the death of Jesus?

One Perspective	Another Perspective
I *[God]* will strike the Shepherd. ...We esteemed Him stricken, smitten by *God*.[41]	My God, My God, why have *You forsaken* Me?[42]

---

[39] Exodus 12:12, NKJV, emphasis supplied.

[40] Exodus 12:23, NKJV, emphasis supplied.

[41] Mark 14:27; Isaiah 53:4, NKJV, emphasis supplied.

[42] Mark 15:34, NKJV, emphasis supplied.

We have already noted that God did not execute Christ, but we still find perplexing language making it appear that He did. What can it mean? We need more background information in order to provide sufficient light on this issue. However, at this point may I suggest a simple governing principle by which to better understand such statements. As we proceed, we shall test its validity:

Principle: *God allows Himself to be portrayed as* doing *what He does not prevent.*

Our God is sovereign. He can do anything He wants to do. Why would He choose to communicate these thoughts in language so foreign to us? Did He actually do these things or not? In some places it appears convincingly that He did, yet in other places it appears that the event occurred without His involvement. This format has produced many thoughtful atheists, agnostics, and perplexed Christians through the years. But it might surprise you to learn that some devout believers throughout history saw this problem and arrived at the same solution for it that I have offered here. In fact, at one time I believed I alone saw this feature of Scripture. But to my surprise I have learned that many Christians of the past have seen this "oddity" and come to the same conclusion as I regarding it.

God allows Himself to be portrayed as doing what He only allows (doesn't prevent). To review many quotations dating from the medieval period that show that Christians through the ages have observed this curiosity and come to some conclusions about it go to https://characterofgod.org/2016/05/i-create-evil/.

Since God could have interposed to prevent any of these incidents from occurring but, for His own reasons, chose not to do so, He is depicted as the actual instrument or performing agent. Notice how often they are described as His actions in vivid, convincing terms. Yet many of these accounts don't make sense in terms of the total picture or in terms of God's character *as Christ modeled it.* It is understandable to wonder if He simply *could have* but *didn't* prevent such incident(s). Is it possible we may have misunderstood and misapplied statements referring to His wrath, anger, or vengeance? We will explore in the chapters ahead the question of why God sometimes "stands down" when He has power to intervene, and, yes, there are even statements in Scripture detailing His feelings when He is obliged to stand down.

Who Was the God of the Old Testament?

We have looked at a few examples of more that I could cite. Can you remember a time when your Bible didn't seem to make sense to you? Did you feel you had to take Scripture on blind faith or feel forced to say this or that action of God's was a good thing when you knew in your heart of hearts that it wasn't? Does it make more sense to you now?

Why would God choose to describe Himself in such a strange way? First, some find it hard to believe that Jesus was the same God found in the Old Testament. "[S]earch the [Old Testament] Scriptures," He said, "[I]t is these that testify about Me."[43] Jesus was the Angel of the Lord, the pillar of cloud by day and fire by night. He was the great I AM. In Exodus 3:13, 14, when God asked Moses to represent Him before Israel and Pharaoh, Moses asked His name, and He gave it as "I AM," the self-existent One. When Jesus claimed that name for Himself in John 8:58, the people, shocked at His apparent presumption, picked up stones to throw at Him.

Again in Genesis, notice how Abraham addressed Him as they negotiated over Sodom. "Will not the Judge of all the earth do right?"[44] Yet the New Testament says, "For not even the Father judges anyone, but He has given all judgment to the Son."[45] Do you see that Jesus was the God who bargained with Abraham about Sodom's fate? Even the New Testament says the Israelite pilgrims drank of the "spiritual rock that followed them, and the rock was Christ."[46] Whenever God the Father appears in the text He is identified as the Ancient of Days, or in some other way He is distinguished from Christ. The rule is that Christ is the God of the Old Testament, unless the text proves otherwise.

Much more is available in the Bible to reveal that of the Heavenly Trio, Jesus was the One who not only came to die for us but who created us and the entire universe as well. Jesus was the God who interacted with humans in the Old Testament. So the question for many is, "What happened to make His character so different in the Incarnation?"

---

[43] John 5:39, NAS.

[44] Genesis 18:25, NKJV.

[45] John 5:22, NAS.

[46] 1 Corinthians 10:4, NSRV.

The answer is: Nothing happened to it. Jesus is the same yesterday, today, and forever.[47] Deity doesn't change. No clearer illustration of the character of Deity has been (or could ever be) given than what is seen in His character when He came as a babe in Bethlehem and grew up among us. Jesus provided a clear demonstration of His Father's love through His life here on earth as a human. That is His real character as well as the character of His Father. Clearly, something is wrong in our understanding of Old Testament views of God. We have missed something.

Everything we read of Him in the Old Testament must be filtered through the demonstration He provided in the New Testament gospels, if we are to better comprehend Him.

Old Testament Structure

Secondly, have you ever noticed how the Old Testament is structured? Most scholars agree that the book of Job was likely written first, then the rest of the manuscripts of the Old Testament. Of those, Job gives explicit attention to the work of Satan. Zechariah 3:1, 2 also briefly mentions Satan by name. First Chronicles 21:1 says that he, Satan, provoked King David to number Israel, and finally, Psalm 109:6 simply says Satan stands at the right hand of the wicked, something of which we should all be aware. Otherwise, the Old Testament barely mentions him. In Isaiah 14 :4,12-17, he is presented as the king of Babylon and in Ezekiel 28:2-19 as the prince or king of Tyre.

This sinister individual who bears responsibility for every bad thing that happens in this world does not receive Old Testament mention comparable to his overwhelming "badness." Even the New Testament speaks of him conservatively, reluctantly, in accordance with the need to warn against him. Why?

Some say it might be due to a writing convention in Bible times to credit everything that happened within the realm to the king, thus marginalizing Satan. It might appear to us, who have no such writing convention, that the king himself actually did what was ascribed to him. This could account somewhat for the strange way Scripture blames God when things go wrong. While it may have appeared perfectly natural to those living in Bible times, it is very confusing to us today.

---

[47] Hebrews 13:8; Malachi 3:6; James 1:17.

Third, God naturally takes the responsibility when things go wrong in His universe, for He is the one who designed and created it to operate on the immutable principles of cause and effect. We saw that He embraced the earth and, when we fell, He gave His Son to provide us a way back to Himself. In contrast, we see Satan who is the "accuser of our brethren,"[48] the very opposite of our wonderful God who is willing to take the blame for things which, from our perspective, He didn't do. What we have failed to realize is the magnitude at which this aspect of His character plays out.

The Blame-taker vs. the Accuser

I can perhaps best illustrate this with a story.

Some time back I worked in an office for a usually very fair-minded man. But one day he got the idea I had not forwarded an important report on its due date. I had no recollection of anyone telling me to send that report out; however, I quickly prepared it for forwarding and wrote a cover memorandum taking full responsibility for its tardiness. When I showed the memorandum to the boss for his approval, he trashed it. "In this office we don't get into blame placing," he said. "As director and manager of this office, I am responsible for all the work that's done here." And he quickly re-wrote the memo.

The story has a happy ending. In a matter of minutes he realized he had looked at the wrong report, which was not supposed to go anywhere, and he graciously apologized to me.

But even as it happened I saw something of God's mind when the boss took the blame. Maturity understands the importance of assuming responsibility, while immaturity blames everything and everyone in sight, seeking to avoid responsibility for fear of punishment. Thus our supremely mature God makes Himself ultimately responsible for the results of granting His intelligent creation free will, even to the extent of assuming responsibility for the numerous episodes of destruction attributed to Him throughout Scripture.

Our heavenly Father wants us to know, He is in charge of His universe. As Creator of heavens and earth and Sustainer of life in the universe, He will never give Satan equal billing with Himself, will never point a finger and say, "He did it, not me!" Since God, out of respect for the freedom of

---

[48] Revelation 12:10, NAS

choice given to all His creation, could have prevented an incident but chose not to do so, He allows Himself to be described as doing it.

Fourth and finally, Scripture may be structured in this way to reveal the power of God. Psalms 24:1 says, "The earth is the Lord's, and all it contains, the world, and those who dwell in it."[49] We cannot imagine how thoroughly dependent we are on God and His power to maintain us in this world. "In Him we live and move and have our being.[50] In the titanic showdown between God and Satan over who is really in charge of our world, our heavenly Father would have us know that nothing is ever truly out of His hands. There is nothing He can't do to bless and benefit us. He carefully guards us day and night until He sees that we prefer another master. When the bad times come and we are crushed beneath life's burdens, He knows that He has power to take those burdens away, but He can't because we have used our free will to try to live apart from Him. Therefore, everything that happens to us as a result of straying from Him, He says He did. He feels that He is responsible. Because every creature lives within the embrace of His sustaining power He is willing to take the blame for all our actions, even though we have complete freedom to operate in any way we prefer, rejecting His ways if we choose.

Satan, too, must rely on the power of God. He can do nothing in his own strength if not kept alive moment to moment by his Creator. He perhaps should have thought of that before he rebelled; he never paused to think how dependent he was upon the power of God to sustain his life. Our "doing" seems such a natural part of us that we feel independently enabled, as though we think things up and can do them on our own, whether taking our first step or performing a complex task. When we make demands on mind or body, the energy seems already to be there. It seems we can go forward on our own without any outside assistance.

This may be why Scripture reminds us of this in the very language we find so puzzling, that God allows Himself to be seen and described as doing what He in His omnipotence could prevent but does not.

This principle is well-known in Scripture and, far from being a modern phenomenon, it has been recognized throughout the ages. Perhaps we can use that principle to give us a better understanding of His character of love.

---

[49] NAS.

[50] Acts 17:28, NKJV.

4

Earth's Invisible Combat

"[W]ar broke out in heaven."
(Revelation 12:7, NKJV)

The history of civilization is a history of war. From ancient battles of forgotten kings to twentieth century superpower conflicts, each succeeding generation has mobilized its armies on the field of confrontation.

This conflict theme pervades the pages of Holy Writ. Its stories make up episodes in a context of warfare on a cosmic scale, and Scripture tells where it all began.

"[W]ar broke out in heaven: Michael and his angels fought against the dragon; and the dragon and his angels fought, but they did not prevail, nor was a place found for them in heaven any longer."[1] Scripture places God's vengeance and the rise and fall of nations within this conflict setting.

Who Were the Angels?
Regarding the good angels Paul the apostle says, "[Angels] are all ministering spirits sent forth to minister for those who will inherit salvation."[2] Since God planned and provided for the salvation of all, we are all recipients of the ministry of holy angels.

---

[1] Revelation 12:7, 8, NKJV, emphasis supplied.

[2] Hebrews 1:14, NKJV.

Zechariah 6 describes four symbolic horse-drawn chariots advancing from before God's throne toward earth, to pass through or patrol the four points of the compass. "Who are they?" asks the prophet.

He learns that they are four "spirits" of heaven. Notice that in Hebrews 1 Paul calls angels "spirits."[3] Psalm 68:17 KJV further verifies that these chariots symbolize angels. "The chariots of God are twenty thousand, even thousands of angels."

By their dispersion to all points of the compass the prophet conveys their presence, though invisible, blanketing our earth. Scripture further affirms, "The angel of the Lord encamps all around those who fear Him, and delivers them."[4] Jesus referred to these angel companions. "Take heed that you do not despise one of these little ones, for I say to you that in heaven their angels always see the face of My Father who is in heaven."[5] Numerous stories, Biblical and otherwise, confirm the presence in our world of an invisible army of beings called angels. One released Peter from prison; another ministered to Jesus in the wilderness of temptation and in Gethsemane. One rolled away the stone from Christ's tomb and called Him forth to life.

Clearly, the Bible depicts our world as a danger zone dependent upon the protecting and ever watchful presence of holy angel visitors. If our eyes could be opened and we could behold the multitude of dangers threatening on every side day and night, we would have a greater sensibility of our debt to God and holy angels for every moment of comfort and joy that we know.

Revelation 7 repeats the prophecy of Zechariah 6, confirming the protecting ministry of angels in our world and expanding their job description to include—destruction.

"I saw four angels standing at the four corners of the earth, holding the four winds of the earth, that the wind should not blow on the earth, on the sea, or on any tree. Then I saw another angel ascending from the east, having the seal of the living God. And He cried with a loud voice to the four angels to whom it was granted to harm the earth and the sea, saying do not harm the earth, the sea or the trees till we have sealed the servants of our God on their foreheads."[6]

---

[3] Hebrews 1:7.

[4] Psalm 34:7 NKJV.

[5] Matthew 18:10 NKJV.

[6] Revelation 7:2, 3 NKJV.

Again, we note four angels positioned at the four points of the compass, signifying their presence everywhere in our world. The Bible often uses the symbol of "winds" to denote strife among men and nations.[7] These mighty angels, in response to orders from the heavenly command center to "Hold," restrain the winds of strife among nations from blowing upon the earth.

Note especially that to these "angels of mercy" is granted power to harm earth and sea. How will they do it? By picking up weapons and going out to kill and destroy? Or could they do it by simply ceasing to protect? Need they do more than release, withdraw, back off from their protecting duties to allow death and chaos to disrupt the social order?

Since these angels take directions from God, and Christ represents God, we may assume that heavenly angels behave as Christ behaved under similar circumstances.

Neither God nor holy angels abandon their protecting duties until thoroughly discharged by their beneficiaries, who, self-sufficient, have never learned their need of utter dependence upon a power outside themselves, never dreamed that a compassionate Providence under-girded all their earthly triumphs. In attitude they say, as Judah said anciently of Christ, "We will not have this Man to reign over us,"[8] never considering that when He is pushed away, His protection goes with Him.

The Dragon and His Angels

The dragon most clearly appears in Revelation 12:1, 9, where he is identified as Satan, the ancient serpent. Other names the Bible gives him are Lucifer, the Adversary, the Accuser, the destroyer, etc.[9] "I will be like the Most High," said Lucifer/Satan; before his fall, son of the morning but turned into "the dragon" afterward.[10] According to the Bible, war began as an ideological conflict between the Creator God and the dragon who aspired to be equal with His office. "In righteousness He [God] doth judge and make war."[11] The weapons in this contest were truth on God's side and deception on the side of His adversary, and when deception could

---

[7] Daniel 7:2; Jeremiah 25:31, 32; 49:36, 37.

[8] Luke 19, 14 NKJV.

[9] Isaiah 14:12, KJV; 1 Peter 5:8; Revelation 12:10; 9:11.

[10] Isaiah 14:1, 14; Revelation 12:1, 9 NKJV.

[11] Revelation 19:11, KJV.

no longer alter the minds of heaven's angels, this Deity wanna-be had to find another home.

Revelation 12 says he persuaded a third of the angels to follow him in rebellion. These are the dragon's angels who fought against the heavenly angels in the original conflict. When those fallen angels lost the war and were "cast out," Jude 6 says they "left" their habitation, yet no where will you read that anyone was "killed." Not so after Lucifer and his host plummeted to our world and the ideological war that commenced in heaven became a synonym for deadly force down here, where it continued with increasing bloodshed. The great conflict began in envy and rages on yet today, not only on fields of earthly battle but also in the daily moral choices in the hearts and minds of every man and woman on this planet.

God's Role
God plays the leading role in the drama, not only as Creator but also as Sustainer of all life and order in the universe. "[God] gives to all mortals life and breath and all things. . . . 'In him we live and move and have our being.'"[12] He sustains life in two ways: first, through the activities of His holy angels as supporting players stationed here with the commission to protect the earth, and secondly, through the presence in the world of His Holy Spirit.

The Holy Spirit
God sustains His creation through the living presence of the Holy Spirit in our world. Scripture abounds in evidence of this. As far back as the Exodus, He said, "I will set My tabernacle among you, and My soul shall not abhor you. I will walk among you and be your God, and you shall be My people."[13] The earthly tabernacle itself, first erected in the wilderness, later assembled at Shiloh and finally expanded at Jerusalem, represented God's living presence with His people, a predominate Scriptural theme.[14]

Many were the symbols through which God sought to teach this truth. "As the mountains surround Jerusalem, so the Lord surrounds His

---

[12] Acts 17:25, 28, NRSV.

[13] Leviticus 26:11, 12, NKJV.

[14] Exodus 25:8.

people."[15] "You have hedged me behind and before."[16] "[T]he reproaches of those who reproach You have fallen on me."[17] The last a prophecy of Christ, also applies to individuals living in God through the Holy Spirit, as He did.

Not only does this picture convey God's ideal for abiding with His people, it describes His plan for protecting them as well. "You have been a shelter for me, and a strong tower from the enemy. I will abide in Your tabernacle forever; I will trust in the shelter of Your wings"; "He who dwells in the secret place of the Most High shall abide under the shadow of the Almighty....He shall cover you with His feathers, and under His wings you shall take refuge."[18]

Nothing is more clear in Scripture than God's plan to live in His people through the Holy Spirit, nor more certain than human dependence upon this connection for salvation and protection. "With favor You will surround Him as with a shield."[19] This concept appears most conspicuously in (but is not limited to) the book of Psalms and the writings of the apostle Paul.

Nature itself depends upon this heavenly ministry to maintain order, generate life, and assure the predictability so essential to the security of life on our planet. So long as God's Spirit and holy angels remain in their appointed place, life continues in familiar patterns. What could ever cause them to depart?

The Conflict of the Ages
In the idyllic glories of heaven, where all is peace and light and every resident finds their greatest joy in praising God, a mystery began to grow in the imagination of the most brilliant angel created, Lucifer, which means bearer of God's light.

Agape, that special kind of other-centered love, permeates the air and guides every relationship and transaction. Besides the Father, Son, Holy Spirit and holy angels, a beautiful angel lived there whose name was Lucifer. He was the "covering angel" before God's throne, leader of the

---

[15] Psalm 125:2, NKJV

[16] Psalm 139:5, NKJV.

[17] Psalm 69:9, NKJV.

[18] Psalms 61:3, 4; 91:1, 4 NKJV.

[19] Psalm 5:12.

celestial choir, a being of unsurpassed beauty, intellect and knowledge above all the creation of God.[20] So long as the lines of other-centeredness remained open, there was peace and harmony and order among heaven's inhabitants. But somehow Lucifer began thinking more about himself instead of looking at God. He saw he was beautiful, wise, and adored by the other angels. Gradually his thoughts began to turn around until finally all Lucifer could focus on was himself. He thought that an angel as beautiful and wise as he, esteemed so highly by the other angels, should really be "like the Most High," and he began to imagine that he should be worshiped as God. Toward this end Lucifer devoted his immense powers of intellect, deceiving other angels who loved him, and leading them to imagine that God was unfair in depriving him of worship. When open rebellion finally erupted, one-third of the angels aligned themselves with him in mutiny against their Maker.

> So the great dragon was cast out, that serpent of old, called the Devil and Satan, who deceives the whole world; he was cast to the earth, and his angels were cast out with him.[21]

Considering the size of the Bible, it is significant that it gives relatively little direct attention to the devil. Because God is a positive Being, He gives this negative creature as little notice as possible, but enough to warn us against him. Sufficient information exists to reveal who he is and what he does. Job 1 and 2, Isaiah 14, Ezekiel 28 and the book of Revelation plus brief statements here and there constitute the body of explicit Scriptural data regarding him.

Having exhausted his welcome in heaven, he later drew the first family of earth into his way of thinking and set up his headquarters here for expanding his reign further in the universe. Although earth's parents, like all other heavenly beings, were created and designed for full other-centeredness, in yielding to this rebel they became distorted to think like him. Their nature was fundamentally changed. Originally created to always seek the good of others, they now readily preferred their own good at the expense of others. Meanwhile in the heavens the rest of the universe waited to see what would happen to a world modeled on self-seeking.

---

[20] Isaiah 14:12; Ezekiel 28:2-5, 12-15; Psalm 99:1 NKJV.

[21] Revelation 12:9, NKJV.

The Fall

God's sense of responsibility appears most striking in contrast with the character of Satan, one of whose names is also called "the accuser."[22] Adam's fall in Eden reveals the involvement of both competing masters. Satan deceived Eve into indulging in the forbidden act, but Adam was not so deceived.[23] He knew his beloved companion would surely die as a result of her transgression; therefore, in desperation he determined to die with her. Note how his love for her at this point faintly reflected the love of God for a fallen human race.

When Adam fell, the quality of his love for Eve instantly changed to reflect that of his new diabolical master. "The woman whom You gave to be with me, she gave me of the tree, and I ate," he said.[24] It was the woman's fault, after all. Or perhaps God, it was Your fault for giving me this defective, seductive woman. It was someone, anyone else's fault, but certainly not mine.

This accusing nature burrowed deep into the gene pool and passed on to the entire human race. For this reason, God calls us to repentance as the very first step back toward His kingdom. Humans cannot see their sin and accept the responsibility apart from the softening influence of the Holy Spirit in their hearts, for it arouses stiff resistance in their fallen nature. Thus God looks for repentance as the first sign of eternal life being reintroduced into the soul. "[T]he wages of sin is death."[25] Thus it has been and ever shall be.

Adam and Eve, through an act of their free will, forfeited their hold on life. The world could have blinked out of existence at that moment had not a voice been heard in heaven saying, "I have found a ransom."[26] The moment sin appeared on the earth, the essence of the cross of Christ appeared simultaneously, for the Lamb of God truly was slain "from the foundation of the world.[27]

God's foreknowledge of a successful revelation of the truth about Himself through the cross of Christ in 31 A. D. allowed Him to unleash

---

[22] Revelation 12:10.

[23] 1 Timothy 2:14.

[24] Genesis 3:12 , NKJV.

[25] Romans 6:23, NKJV.

[26] Job 33:24, NKJV.

[27] Revelation 13:8, NKJV.

the power in that cross at the very moment sin appeared on the earth. The cross of Christ, an emblem of both God's mercy and justice, has power to hold the world in check while humanity was provided a second chance. But second chances don't last forever.

Before heaven can finally bring an end to the reign of sin, certain issues must be settled. How much does God really love His creatures, and can love be trusted in the face of violence? Are God's ways trustworthy when it appears they are so weak against the stern realities of life under the enormous pressures of selfishness and greed? Could anything be salvaged from this deeply damaged planet? Would it even be possible for fallen humans to be transformed enough to receive God's love and reflect it into their world filled with so much dysfunction? If a way might be found to do it, would such ones be willing to say goodbye to sin forever and be cured of their deep investment in Satan's reward/punishment model? While the universe awaits the answers, the work of the Holy Spirit goes on and God's angels hold back the winds of strife, thus "capping" sin's natural effects. But when in the last days iniquity abounds and God is compelled to give the command "Release," the universe will witness how fast sin will self-destruct.

The Destroyer

The Bible pictures Lucifer, meaning light bearer, whose name was changed to Satan, the accuser, depicting his radical change in character as a liar and deceiver. It also calls him "the destroyer," and Jesus identified him as a murderer from the beginning, a point vital to our present study. Scripture frequently mentions the destroyer, but in order to verify his identity, we must return to Revelation, this time to 9:1, 11: "I saw a star fallen from heaven to the earth. And to him was given the key to the bottomless pit." "And they had as king over them the angel of the bottomless pit, whose name in Hebrew is Abaddon, but in Greek he has the name Apollyon."[28]

Both names, Abaddon and Apollyon, mean "destroyer." The following parallel texts clearly identify this "fallen star":

• "How are you fallen from heaven, O Lucifer, son of the morning....Yet you shall be brought down to Sheol, to the lowest depths of the pit."[29]

---

[28] NKJV.

[29] Isaiah 14:12 NKJV.

• "I saw Satan fall like lightning from heaven."[30]

• "So the great dragon was cast out [of heaven], that serpent of old, called the Devil and Satan"[31]

Isaiah 14 continues, You "made the world as a wilderness and destroyed its cities,"[32] destroyed the land and slew the people. Close comparison of Revelation 9 with Isaiah 14:12-20 and Revelation 12 leaves little question that the "destroyer" of Revelation 9:11 is Satan himself. Do we even need ask why God finds it necessary to shelter us in the face of this death machine?

In other statements of Scripture, God says, "My Spirit shall not always strive with man," and "grieve not the holy Spirit."[33] King David, following his dual sin of adultery and murder, prayed, "Do not take Your Holy Spirit from me."[34] Scripturally it is clear that it is possible to send the Holy Spirit away from us. So what determines whether God, His Holy Spirit, and angel representatives stay or leave us alone? Much in our study depends on the answer to this pivotal question.

Obedience Grants Authority

"Do you not know that when you present yourselves to someone as slaves for obedience, you are slaves of the one whom you obey, either of sin resulting in death, or of obedience resulting in righteousness?"[35]

In response to the charges of Satan and in harmony with His commitment to protecting our free will, God has agreed to let humans make their own decision as to who will be their spiritual master. Since we naturally are more concerned about ourselves than others, we are by nature children of "wrath," as the Bible calls it.[36] Satan has us enslaved by defaulting Adam's choice to compromise the entire human race. God countered with the power of love unveiled at the cross.

---

[30]Luke 10:18, NKJV.

[31] Revelation 12:7, NKJV.

[32] NKJV.

[33] Genesis 6:3; Ephesians 4:30, KJV.

[34] Psalm 51:11, NKJV.

[35] Romans 6:16, NAS.

[36] Ephesians 2:3.

When a person or a people refuse irreversibly to surrender to all that God has done to win their trust in Him at the cross, when their lives reveal deliberate defiance and indifference to God's expressed will, when God has exhausted His complete arsenal of love in every effort to draw them to His eternal life and they refuse to respond, Satan then declares himself the victor in their lives. According to the terms of the great contest between God and Satan over their allegiance, our sovereign God must limit His authority and restrain His power to intervene for them. The reality is not that He *will not* rescue them, but rather He *cannot* move on their behalf without their permission. When people have cast Him off, when their free-will decisions are finalized and the gentle wooing of His Spirit no longer is heard to affect them, when they have thrown away the gift of repentance until it becomes impossible to feel it, then they have given themselves over irreversibly to the kingdom of darkness and Satan stakes his claim over their souls. Their heart is then no longer able to respond to God's love, for their conscience has now been seared with a hot iron.[37]

The Possible Meaning of Disasters
It is interesting to speculate occasionally on how this understanding might help explain events occurring around us in the world today. In that connection, on October 10, 1986, the [Boise] *Idaho Statesman* newspaper published an article on the nuclear production reactor at Hanford, Washington, stating, "At 5:30 a.m. a highly concentrated plutonium solution was transferred from one holding tank to another....Only after the transfer had been made did someone realize that a pipe linking the second tank to a third tank was still connected. If the concentrated plutonium solution had entered the third tank, the liquid could have gone 'critical,' the point at which a nuclear chain reaction takes place....A series of six valves that had remained closed throughout the incident prevented the transfer of liquid. Still the episode—one of fifty-four 'criticality' incidents at Hanford dating back two years—was so disturbing that the U.S. Department of Energy took the unprecedented step October 8 of indefinitely shutting down the plant." Except for site cleanup, it is still closed over two decades later with no plans to reopen.

---

[37] 1Timothy 4:2.

Did a heavenly angel hand secure those six valves? What could happen to such valves if our protector God loses authority over them in His deference to human free will?

Climate change cannot fully explain the increase in the number and strength of natural disasters occurring around the world today. Our planet trembles under the ferocity of tornadoes and hurricanes which repeatedly slam coastal cities killing thousands and leaving hundreds of thousands homeless and destitute. Volcanoes dormant for centuries awaken, their fire and brimstone breath threatening communities which have for generations lived peacefully on their fertile slopes. Does a connection exist between earth's burgeoning sin problem and its increase in natural disasters—both in number and ferocity?

The thought of invisible intelligences monitoring the collective decisions and attitudes of earth life may sound like the figment of a screenwriter's imagination, yet scientific insights cannot rule it out.

Lincoln Barnett writing in *The Universe and Dr. Einstein*, points out a fact well known both in and out of the world of science, that human sensory equipment cannot begin to register all that takes place around us in our world. Referring only to the sense of sight, he says, "The human eye fails to respond to most of the 'lights' in the world and . . . what man can perceive of the reality around him is distorted and enfeebled by the limitations of his organ of vision. The world would appear far different to him if his eye were sensitive, for example, to x-rays."[38]

In response to the question of what is "real" in our world, he says, "It is as though the true objective world lies forever half concealed beneath a translucent, plastic dome. Peering through its cloudy surface, deformed and distorted by the ever-changing perspectives of theory, man faintly espies certain apparently stable relationships and recurring events. A consistent isomorphic representation of these relationships and events is the maximal possibility of his knowledge. Beyond that point he stares into the void."[39]

Knowing how little we know makes more plausible the reality of an invisible world of which Scripture tells, occupied by demons and holy angels, whispering their temptations and prompting us to

---

[38] 2d ed. (Harper & Brothers, 1957), p. 13.

[39] *Ibid*, pp. 114-5.

holiness, a parallel world where the Holy Spirit in the persona of Christ walks and talks with the blessed who do not resist His entreaties.

Our world, seemingly so immediate and palpable to us, holds dimensions of reality into which our senses cannot penetrate. Higher levels of creatures watch our world, observing the contest between moral soundness and perversity. In this vast theater one absolute rule prevails: Humans choose their own master through their own behavior patterns. They cannot manipulate a different outcome than that which flows naturally from their own moral choices. They cannot remain neutral. Neither side will forfeit their authority over anyone unless the person makes the choice to change sides.

How Does God Destroy?

The two powers in charge of the contest possess opposite characters. With One, the direction of attention flows out. God's word reveals Him as totally other-centered, totally supportive, totally creative, redemptive, healing, compassionate, and selfless. The other is described as the destroyer, his whole purpose being to deceive and exploit, thereby to destroy. No one ever argues that Satan redeems. Yet it has often appeared to us as if God destroys. But those who are wise, who see the problems with the traditional view of a destroying God, will ask the question: How does He do it?

The Bible invariably describes God's destructive acts in terms amenable to human perception. But we have noted the inadequacy of human senses to pick up on the larger perspective.

The Biblical story of the plagues of Egypt suggests a deeper level of destructive activity than appears on the surface. Designed to induce Pharaoh to free the Hebrew slaves, the plagues afford another of those puzzling apparent contradictions in Scripture. You will recall they consisted of waters turned to blood, frogs overrunning the land, lice taking over, flies to the max, diseased livestock, painful boils on man and beast, hail, locusts, and finally the tragic deaths of every firstborn child.[40]   In each case the language suggests that God, by personal imposition, inflicted these disasters on the heads of the hapless Egyptians.

---

[40] Exodus 7:14—12:30.

"For *I* will pass through the land of Egypt on that night, and will strike all the firstborn in the land of Egypt, both man and beast; and against all the gods of Egypt *I* will execute judgment: *I am the Lord.*"[41]

The surface message here seems to suggest that since the Egyptians' sinfulness had gone too far, God personally executed their firstborn in order to persuade Pharaoh to release the Hebrews from slavery. Yet the Bible contains a number of specific references to these plagues which hint of something very different occurring beyond human vision than we see from our surface view:

Who killed the firstborn of Egypt?

One Perspective	Another Perspective
God speaking: "For *I* will pass through the land of Egypt on that night and will strike all the firstborn in the land of Egypt, both man and beast; against all the gods of Egypt *I will execute judgment: I am the Lord.*"[41]	"For the Lord will pass through to strike the Egyptians: and when He sees the blood on the doorposts the Lord will pass over the door and not allow *the destroyer* to come into your houses to strike you."[42]

Notice the quotation on the right carefully. It suggests *two* actors in that terrible drama: "The Lord" and "the destroyer." If the Lord does not see the blood, He will come down. Why? To strike (as we would express it)? No. To "allow" the destroyer to strike.

An Illustration

Regarding this final Egyptian plague, God gave careful instructions that only homes with the blood of an animal sprinkled on their doorposts, representing faith in the death of Christ yet future, would escape the terrible curse. Thus began the Passover, the first of the traditional feasts of Israel.

God speaks to us where we are and through the aspects of our culture with which we have become most familiar. The Hebrews at the time of the

---

[41] Exodus 12:12 NKJV, emphasis supplied.

[42] Exodus 12:23 NKJV, emphasis supplied.

Exodus had a long history of respecting binding covenants. The Threshold Covenant on which Passover is modeled came down through time from the much respected family altar of antiquity, and it is still observed today in the nations of the East. Anciently, the family altar took place at the residence's threshold. The host sprinkled the blood of a slain lamb or other animal over the threshold, thus the threshold took on great religious significance. Anyone inside the house having passed over the sprinkled animal blood on the threshold was under the sponsorship and care of the host. It was the most secure place to be in the realm. Perhaps due to Israel's familiarity with the Threshold Covenant, God chose to pattern the first rites of the Hebrew nation, the Passover, on it.[43] God through Moses instructed the people to take an unblemished male first-year lamb, slay it on the fourteenth day, and strike the blood on the two side posts and the upper door post of their homes. All who sought refuge inside the house, including Egyptians, were safe from the tenth plague, the death of all the firstborn in the land of Egypt.

Let us then picture two homes standing side by side on that night, one with the blood, one without. The midnight hour arrives. Invisibly God's "death angel" appears, carrying in its hands the destroying weapon from the supernatural realm. He looks at one house, sees the blood and passes over. He sees no blood on the house next door, and he comes down. What does he carry in his hand? Is that a sword? Perhaps a laser or a lightning bolt? No. It is a document on which is stamped the name of God. He shows it to the guardian angel, throughout the years stationed at the door of the house devoid of the saving blood. "Release," says the document. Together the angels fly away, exposing the firstborn within to the destroyer, waiting eagerly without. Notice, please, that Egypt had received abundant warnings that they were dealing with the great God of Israel. The Egyptians knew by this time that their gods were no match for Jehovah. God gave them a way of escape from this terrible plague, and some took advantage of it.

The next chapter looks at what limits the destroyer from accessing the firstborn who took refuge under the blood. Notice that this perspective agrees with the way in which God dealt with sin in the case of Christ the Sin Bearer.

---

[43] H. Clay Trumbull, *The Threshold Covenant* or *The Beginning of Religious Rites*. Project Gutenberg. http://gutenberg.org, 6/14/2015

Did the Father play a role in the death of Jesus?

One Perspective	Another Perspective
"I[God] will strike the Shepherd. ... [W]e esteemed Him *stricken, smitten* by God."[44]	"My God, My God, why have You *forsaken* Me?"[45]

In each case God backs off, releasing entrenched sinners over to the destroyer's power. In each case He sees and describes Himself as "striking" or doing what in actuality He merely allows.

The book of Psalms has a final word to say regarding this terrible experience, faintly underscoring our new model of the episode of the plagues and calling into question our traditional presumptions about God's participation in them:

> *He cast on them the fierceness of His anger,[w]rath, indignation, and trouble, [b]y sending angels of destruction among them. He made a path for His anger; He did not spare their soul from death, [b]ut gave their life over to the plague, [a]nd destroyed all the firstborn in Egypt.[46]*

As Christ was *delivered up*, so Egypt was *given over* to destruction. The evidence mounts that God destroys in a way very different from the way in which Satan or humans destroy. It suggests He withdraws—simply and reluctantly—removing His protecting, life-giving shield in compliance with and respect for human free moral choices.

God expressed His "anger, wrath, indignation, and trouble" through the plagues, including the destruction of the firstborn. In the next chapter we shall examine a previously overlooked Biblical definition of these terms which supports the alternate model we have introduced here.

---

[44] Mark 14:27 NKJV, Isaiah 53:4 NKJV, emphasis supplied.

[45] Mark 15:34 NKJV; Psalm 22:1 NKJV, emphasis supplied

[46] Psalm 78:49, 50, NKJV.

5

The Job Syndrome

"'Shall we indeed accept good from God, and shall we not accept adversity?' In all this Job did not sin with his lips." (Job 2:10)

A side from the gospels, the story of Job is one of the most interesting in the Biblical narrative. Limitations of time and space preclude us from exploring the many facets that make this story so fascinating. We will confine our study to the first section that took place in the invisible world, because it sets up the action of the remainder of the book.

Job's Test

> There was a man in the land of Uz whose name was Job; that man was blameless and upright, one who feared God and shunned evil.[1]

Thus begins the book of Job, traditionally held to be the first written of those collected in the Holy Bible. Whether the tradition is true or not, it seems fitting that it should be, because the book of Job deals with the oldest questions of all: Why? What is God's role and purpose in human suffering? Why do the righteous suffer? Humans have asked these questions since the beginning of time; how like God to have provided insights to address them long ago in the book of Job.

---

[1] Job 1:1, NKJV.

75

There is a tradition that Moses, under divine inspiration, wrote the book of Job. I tend to believe this is true, because only God could open up to us what was going on behind the scenes in the world normally invisible to human eyes. Job never received that information. As far as we know, he never understood why or how this adversity came to him.

Then we learn that Satan presented himself before the heavenly council as the representative of this earth. He and God exchange comments regarding Job, and God says, So you say humans cannot avoid sin? Have you noticed my righteous servant Job?

Yes, says Satan, but you've hedged him around with protective angels. He obeys you for the benefits. Just let me at him, and he'll blame You and curse You to Your face. God says, You're wrong, Satan. Job serves Me because He knows and loves Me.

They agree to a test to prove who is right. Poor Job! All he can see are his children destroyed, his livestock stolen, his body transformed into a mass of loathsome sores. He sees no more than we can ordinarily see when we read Scriptural accounts of destructive acts attributed to God. Job's senses cannot penetrate into the invisible world. But in this instance we are given an advantage over Job. We can see with greater clarity, because God has opened to us this drama occurring in the heavenly realms. We have what writers call the "omniscient" viewpoint. Here the curtain draws aside, revealing the actors within the invisible world itself; therefore, we know Why, and we know How.

Our Emotional God

Although in describing the events of that meeting in the invisible world little emotion seems evident, future events reveal that God felt great emotion as He discussed with the Accuser His friend Job that day, for as it turned out, He (God) was about to release His wrath on Job.

One definition of *Strong's Exhaustive Concordance of the Bible* reveals His wrath to be strong, passionate emotion. The wrath of God involves intense emotions whenever He allows destructive things to happen to His cherished people, in fact, to any of His children. *Strong's* definition connects his wrath to "rapid breathing in passion," suggesting that wrath calls out God's emotions as nothing else can do. He says, "I was crushed by their wanton heart that turned away from me,"[2] and "How

---

[2] Ezekiel 6:9, NRSV, emphasis supplied.

often they rebelled against . . . [Me] in the wilderness and grieved . . . [Me] in the desert! They tested God again and again, and provoked the Holy One of Israel."[3] We have too often glossed over the many statements in Scripture which, if we would pause to notice them, would reveal God to be extremely emotional. Hurt or destruction coming on His people is a great wounding hardship for God, for when He sees His people hurt, it is as if the disaster has touched Him as well.

The book of Job contains more references to "wrath" than any other book in the Biblical narrative, which shows that although Job didn't understand why this was happening to him, he nonetheless recognized that it was the wrath of God. Some examples are, "He tears me in His wrath."[4] "He kindles His wrath against me,"[5] and "Oh, that You would hide me in the grave, [t]hat You would conceal me until Your wrath is past."[6]

In agreeing to this challenge from the Adversary, our God positioned Himself to experience much grief and sorrow until the present issue was settled and indeed until the conflict is over forever and the victory won. The book of Job will forever remain a significant episode is that conflict.

The remaining chapters find the protagonist tragically reduced in fortune and engaged in philosophical debate with some so-called friends, trying to make sense of this disaster.

Job's Response To Wrath

In response to his friends' insistence that God blesses the righteous and punishes the wicked, Job says, "Who does not know such things as these? . . . I know it is so. . . . What you know I also know; I am not inferior to you."[7] He seems to have agreed rather than disagreed with his friends on the basic rule that God blesses His own and curses His enemies.

If Job believed as his friends believed, interpreting prosperity as a signal of God's favor, then in what respect was he right and they wrong, as the book's ending clearly shows? Job says, "God has *delivered me* to the ungodly, and *turned me over* to the hands of the wicked."[8] Job's friends

---

3 Psalm 78:40, NRSV, emphasis supplied.

4 Job 16:9, NKJV, emphasis supplied. 5

Job 19:11, NKJV, emphasis supplied. 6

Job 14:13,NKJV, emphasis supplied. 7

Job 12:3; 9:2; 13:2, NKJV.

8 Job 16:11, NKJV, emphasis supplied.

seemed not to understand something that Job clearly understood: Sometimes for a redemptive purpose God, temporarily and in a limited way, exposes His own to trouble, a situation I call "the Job Syndrome." Job, knowing himself, was perhaps in a better position than they to see this truth. God's conclusion? Job spoke the truth about Him.[9]

The Hedge
Did you notice the first thing that was needed when God allowed Satan to afflict Job? He lowered the hedge around him. With that protective covering or garment or shield in place, as the Adversary observed, nothing could get through to harm Job. For an interesting exercise go through the Bible and see how many references you can find to this protective covering. What do you think it is? What does it mean to you?

A Template
When we are confronted with adversity for which we can find no explanation, we might hold up the book of Job as a template to help us better understand what might be happening.

The Wrath of God
While Job seemed to comprehend, at least to some degree, the dynamics of "the wrath of God." Christians have generally viewed it as a punishment God personally administers when He gets angry. He's been patient ever so long, but humans have spurned His grace—He can't reach them any more. We have tied logic in knots trying to explain how a God who never stops loving, whose grace never stops flowing, can also be a god who rains fire, drops humans into cracks in the earth or drowns them! Job seemed to understand there is more to the "wrath of God" than meets the eye.

Here as in so many cases of heavenly truth, we must remain open to reversing our traditional understandings or presumptions. When we objectively allow the Bible to explain itself, we discover that the wrath of God is another of the apparent paradoxes of Scripture and that it is the diametric opposite of our usual way of thinking. The following references reveal that the wrath (or indignation or fury or anger) of God occurs by His *withdrawing* from a person or people because (except in the case of

---

[9] Job 42:7, NKJV.

"The Job Syndrome") they have made an irrevocable decision to continue in a course of willful sin, thus depriving Him of authority to involve Himself in their affairs. God's absence then leaves that person or people vulnerable to the the attacks of the destroyer or to the consequences of violated natural principles. While numerous references in virtually all books of the Bible support this position, most of them contain only two or three of the four elements in the code, which I have dubbed "Another Bible Code." The following references contain all four elements:

Another Bible Code

1. [Because sin is chosen]

2. God withdraws

3. Results in trouble

4. And /equals His wrath/

Then My /anger/ shall be aroused against them in that day,and I will **forsake** them, and I will **hide My face** from them, and they shall be *devoured*. And many *evils and troubles* shall befall them, so that they will say in that day, "Have not these *evils* come upon us because our **God is not among us**?" And I will surely **hide My face** in that day because of all the [evil] which they have done, in that [they have turned to other gods].[10]

I will *slay* in My /anger/ and My /fury/ all for whose [wickedness] I have **hidden My face** from this city.[11]

For our fathers have [trespassed] and done [evil] in the eyes of the Lord our God. . . . Therefore the /wrath/ of the Lord fell upon Judah and Jerusalem, and he has **given them up** to *trouble*...[12]

[They caused their sons and daughters to pass through the fire, practiced witchcraft and soothsaying, and sold themselves to do evil] in the sight of the Lord, to provoke Him to /anger/. Therefore, the Lord was very /angry/ with Israel, and **removed them from His sight**. . . . .The

---

[10] Deuteronomy 31:17,18, NKJV.

[11] Jeremiah 33::5, NKJV.

[12] 2 Chronicles 29: 6, 8, NKJV.

79

Lord rejected all the descendants of Israel, *afflicted* them, and *delivered them into the hand of plunderers*, until He had **cast them from His sight.**[13]

For the [iniquity of his covetousness] I was /angry/ and *struck* him; **I hid** and was /angry/.[14]

For the Lord will *strike* Israel, as a reed is shaken in the water. He will uproot Israel from this good land which He gave to their fathers, and will *scatter* them beyond the River, because they have [made their wooden images] provoking the Lord to /anger/. And He will **give Israel up** [because of the sins of Jeroboam], who [sinned] and who [made Israel sin].[15]

Job does not fit the pattern these quotations suggest; he suffered though he was righteous. But compare these texts with the experience of Jesus, the great Sin-bearer, when God "made him to be sin for us."[16] Does Jesus' experience agree or disagree with these few texts and many others like them? The Father did not exempt His Son from the darkness of sin's consequences. But it was *our* sins He bore, *our* death He died.

The Bible speaks of the "defiling" of the earth itself.[17] Could this refer to God's losing authority over a specific geographic location in deference to the choice of humans residing there to separate from Him through sin? God lets us choose His kingdom or ours. He will respect that choice. We are accountable for what we know and what we *can* know, if we will open our eyes and look.[18] When humans spurn God's grace irretrievably, Satan stakes a claim on their soul. If we have failed in our lives to provide God with arguments against Satan's claims, if our lives show no genuine commitment to the principles of heaven, what else can God do? What can He say? Since God sees our vulnerability apart from His loving

---

[13] 2 Kings 17:17-20, NKJV.

[14] Isaiah 57:17, NKJV.

[15] 1 Kings14:15, 16, NKJV. For those wishing to explore this topic further I recommend Ray Foucher's website (https://characterofgod.org/2016/02/wrath-of-god/), which claims to have found more than seventy Bible texts giving all four elements of this code.

[16] 2 Corinthians 5:21, KJV.

[17] See, for example, Isaiah 24:5; Psalm 106:38; Numbers 35:33, 34.

[18] John 9:41.

omnipotence, in the most emphatic language at times, He says He *does* what human free will has deprived Him of authority to prevent. All He has really done, all He can do, is sadly withdraw, acknowledging that the human decision is final.

Note that in Scriptural accounts of destructive acts attributed to God, we "see" only the results; we do not "see" the means. Therefore, patterning God after ourselves[19] we have assumed He destroys as we would destroy. But might not our God, knowing He has the power to prevent a disaster, feel the same burden of responsibility as if He had administered the blow Himself? In the language of Scripture He takes the blame, as He took the blame on Calvary so long ago. Satan is the accuser; God, by contrast, has always said, Let the blame fall on Me.

But what of Job? He certainly had not rejected God out of his life. Rather, Job can be viewed as a symbol of Christ, a righteous man whom God allowed to be treated as a sinner in order to fulfill a necessary, redemptive purpose. God honored Job in allowing this patient man to vindicate Him against the challenge of the prince of darkness—to demonstrate that his loyalty to God had nothing to do with his fortunes—a purpose which Job would likely have approved had he known about it. When Job had passed the test at last, here is what Scripture says of him: "[T]he Lord restored Job's losses when he prayed for his friends. Indeed the Lord gave Job twice as much as he had before."[20] Similarly, Jesus, the Pattern Man, received blessings in His life after passing *His* test for "God also has highly exalted Him and given Him the name which is above every name, that at the name of Jesus every knee should bow, . . . " and "every tongue…confess that Jesus Christ is Lord."[21]

Principles of Living

Consideration of the reasons for suffering would be incomplete without mentioning the role of law in human fortune. Consequences exist for law breaking, and laws or principles exist governing our health, our interpersonal relationships, our finances, over virtually every area of human endeavor. When we break the laws or principles by which these systems operate, we may suffer the consequences. But it is most unkind

---

[19] Psalm50:21.

[20] Job 42:10, NKJV.

[21] Philippians 2:9,10, NKJV.

and inaccurate to blame God for our suffering in cases such as these. In fact, I suspect we might be surprised if we knew how often God has shielded us from the results of our own folly and transgressions. But should we expect Him to continue this, once we have come to clearly understand the underlying issues?

Now let us compare the message of Job with our deeper insights into God's character:

> 1. Satan, the destroyer, is the executor of human suffering. Period. The ancient book of Job teaches this convincingly.

> 2. When entrenched sin deprives God of authority to shield, He has no option but to release the protecting "hedge."[22]

> 3. God sets the boundaries for Satan's destructive work.[23] He did in limiting Satan's access to only Job's possessions at first and then to his body, sparing Job's life. He did so similarly in Egypt, limiting the destroyer to the lice, frogs, etc., and to Egypt's firstborn. At world's end however, His judgments will fall "without mixture" or dilution with mercy, without limit.[24]   (This exposes the fact that God has limited the destroyer's activities, as mentioned in Chapter 4, "Earth's Invisible Combat.")

> 4. God takes the blame. He sees and describes Himself as doing what He does not prevent.

Does God Break His Promise?

God has promised that He will never leave or forsake us,[25] and we hear it said so often that we know a great many of God's children lean heavily on it. We sometimes think that because God is love, when we profess to belong to him we should have never-ending good in our lives. At least, we feel God should always be there for us. But how do we account for the many examples where God appears to leave? where His favor is withdrawn? We have included many stories in this book and there are many, many others. How do we understand when our personal life goes

---

[22] Job 1:10.

[23] Job 1:12; 2:6.

[24] Revelation14:10, KJV.

[25] Hebrews 13:5.

topsy-turvy, when hurricanes come and handicapped babies are born and someone else gets the promotion we expected? How are we to understand God's love and His nearness to us at such times?

God is truly love and His promise is rock-solid. He will never, never, never leave us. But I fear we have not seen the complete Bible picture regarding this because we have not searched out the *other texts* that bear on this issue. For example, how are we to understand such texts as,

"[T]he Lord is with you when you are with Him. And if you seek Him, He will let you find Him; but if you forsake Him, He will forsake you."[26] What are the circumstances under which the God of love appears to leave us?

As many examples in this book show, He has appeared at times to back away from His promise, and peoples and nations have disappeared because of it. In order to understand this subject we must review how God communicates with us in the first place. He communicates with us today primarily through the Holy Scriptures; therefore, we can and should acquire a good working knowledge of His ways as revealed in Scripture.

But He also communicates with us through His Spirit. This aspect of His character needs to be better understood if we are to comprehend His promise not to leave or forsake us. If that voice becomes faint and we go on doing our own thing in spite of the Holy Spirit's promptings, we can come to the place where we don't hear Him any more. Eventually our worldly desires drown out the Spirit's voice. Then it matters not where God is; He could be close beside us but we would not perceive it. That is when the dragon-voiced destroyer is permitted to come in and stake his claim upon the soul. So in reality who left who? Was it God? or was it the human who was indifferent to whether God was with Him or not? a human who carelessly failed to cherish His presence?

I believe God weeps when we compel Him to depart from us, whether by an individual or by a nation. But I also believe that one can know with a level of assurance when he or she is safely protected in the center of His will.

What about the suffering Christian. Does someone who lives very close to God, who conscientiously daily does His will, never suffer? If he does suffer does that mean that God has left that person or forsaken him? What about where tragedy strikes a child of God as in the story of Job?

---

[26] 2 Chronicles 15:2, NAS.

83

Jesus Himself passed through such a time as well as many martyrs through the ages. This is what I call "the Job Syndrome," where we can't think of what we have done to displease Him, yet we suffer. These experiences call for trust; a determination to believe that God is somehow working for good while letting us pass through a time of deep darkness. When we face such times in our life, God asks us to hang on to Him, to keep believing and keep praising Him for His love and goodness.

Then whatever the outcome, we can know that He loves us, that He is still with us, working out the good He has promised in our lives.

Never forget that powerful weapon of praise God has given us to use when our fortunes seem to be "going south." At such times sincere praise can often turn the tide, as in the invisible world Satan flees at the sound of praise. I've seen it happen too many times to doubt it. And since praise is such a formidable weapon when circumstances threaten, it is that much more powerful when things are going right. So lift up your voice, fellow Christians, and praise our God and King! Nothing panics Satan and his forces more than hearing praise to the living God from His humble servants on earth. Nothing brings the living God into the circle of our being and circumstances more than praise! With praise His promise is assured: "I will never leave thee or forsake thee."

God truly is always with us. But He has given us freedom, and we, through neglect or conscious exercise of our free will, have the option to leave Him. Yet when we leave Him, it often appears that God has left us! As humans fall for his lies, Satan relentlessly asserts his rights to enforce his harsh principles when humans take his side in the great conflict of the ages. God is then compelled to stand back. What else can He do? Though supremely powerful, God is also courteous, and His respect for our freedom of choice means that He is compelled by the rules of the great conflict to step back when we refuse to give Him authority in our lives. Yet when we read about such times in the Bible, it depicts His actions as His taking the initiative. A careful survey of Scripture, however, confirms it is not really so, rather, that it was humans who have left Him.

In this connection, here is more data for our familiar chart:

Who assaulted Job?

One Perspective	Another Perspective
Satan says: "Stretch out *Your* hand and touch all that he has, and he will surely curse *You* to *Your* face!"[27] After Satan's first assault against Job, God said to Satan, "[Y]ou incited *Me* against him to destroy him without cause."[28]	"Behold, all that he has is in *your* [*Satan's*] power."[29]

Here we catch God in the very act of accepting blame for destruction He only allowed. Comparing this with the loss of Egypt's firstborn, we have . . .

Who destroyed
the firstborn of Egypt?

One Perspective	Another Perspective
"*I [God]* will pass through the land of Egypt on that night, and will strike all the firstborn in the land of Egypt, both man and beast; and against all the gods of Egypt *I* will execute judgment: *I am the Lord.*"[30]	"For the Lord will pass through to strike the Egyptians; and when He sees the blood on the lintel and on the two doorposts, the Lord will pass over the door and not allow *the destroyer* to come into your houses to strike you."[31]

. . . and with the death of Christ:

---

[27] Job 1:11, NKJV

[28] Job 2:3 , NKJV.

[29] Job 1:12, NKJV.

[30] Exodus 12:12, NKJV, emphasis supplied.

[31] Exodus 12:23, NKJV, emphasis supplied.

Did God the Father kill Jesus?

One Perspective	Another Perspective
"*I* [God the Father] will *strike* the Shepherd."[32]	"My God, My God, why have *You forsaken* Me?"[33]

Further, look what the writer of the book of Job said when the ordeal was over and Job had been restored. "They [his family] comforted and consoled him over all the trouble *the Lord* had brought upon him."[34] There is a sense in which this is a true statement, but it is certainly not the whole story.

Insights from Job fully support the idea that God does not destroy as humans destroy. Rather, destruction is a result of the withdrawal of His protection, releasing humans to whatever fate may await them outside His protective authority. Yet He sees and describes Himself as doing what He sadly permits, thus validating our hypothesis.

The book of Job reveals a world usually closed to human vision. Other examples of God's wrath limit us to sensory evidence. Does the traditional picture based on sensory descriptions give the full account? Or do we find in the story of Job principles applying not just to a single event in antiquity but to much if not all of human adversity throughout time?

---

[32] Mark 14:27; Isaiah 53:4, NKJV, emphasis supplied.

[33] Mark 15:34, NKJV, emphasis supplied.

[34] Job 42:11, NKJV, emphasis supplied.

6

Some Fatal Examples

"He that loveth not knoweth not
God; for God is love."
(1 John.4.8)

By now you may be looking at such statements as the following with new eyes:

> "See, O Lord and consider! To whom have You done this? Should the women eat their offspring, [t]he children they have cuddled? Should the priest and prophet be slain in the sanctuary of the Lord?...You have slaughtered and not pitied. You have invited as to a feast day [t]he terrors that surround me. In the day of the Lord's *anger* [t]here was no refugee or survivor."[1]

You now have the tools to review some classic Bible descriptions of God's wrath and see things you may not have seen before:

- "Uzza put out his hand to hold the ark. . . . Then the *anger* of the Lord was aroused against Uzza, and He *struck* him because he put his hand to the ark, and he died there before God."[2]

- "That same night the angel of Yahweh went out and *struck* down a hundred and eighty-five thousand men in the Assyrian camp."[3]

---

[1] Lamentations 2:20-22, NKJV, emphasis supplied.

[2] 1 Chronicles 13:9, 10, NKJV, emphasis supplied.

[3] Isaiah 37:36, JB; 2 Kings 19:35, JB, emphasis supplied

- "[W]hile the meat was still between their teeth…the *wrath* of the Lord was aroused against the people, and the Lord *struck* the people with a very great plague.…[T]here they buried the people who had yielded to craving."[4]

- "Then Ananias…fell down and breathed his last.…Then immediately she [Sapphira] fell down…and breathed her last."[5]

If the meaning of God's wrath in other places is His removing Himself from the arena of willful, entrenched sin, why isn't it here? If God's striking the firstborn of Egypt, the patriarch Job, and His own Son entailed releasing them to the power of the destroyer, why isn't it the same here? and other places as well? Would not the results—perceivable evidence—be the same, whether He personally strikes or simply releases sinners to whatever fate awaits them outside Himself? If we cannot agree that God's role in all these incidents is consistent and in keeping with His changelessness,[6] we must assume the burden of proving it is not.

Further, note what took place when God struck Miriam with leprosy:

So the anger *of the Lord was aroused against them, and He* departed. *And when the cloud* departed *from above the tabernacle, suddenly Miriam became leprous, as white as snow.*[7]

What did God do when he became *angry*? He *departed*. Only then did Miriam appear leprous.

Shiloh

Another revealing incident surrounds loss of Israel's first religious center at Shiloh. Eli, the High Priest, did not properly discipline his sons, also priests, and as a result their wayward example led Israel into spiritual declension. Their influence weakened national defenses to the extent they suffered a great military defeat to the Philistines. Then someone got a "great" idea.

---

[4] Numbers 11:33, 34, NKJV, emphasis supplied.

[5] Acts 5:5, 10, NKJV.

[6] See Malachi 3:6; Hebrews 13:6, James 1:17.

[7] Numbers 12:10, NKJV, emphasis supplied.

Let's bring the ark of the covenant out to war with us. It will bring victory. They had begun to view the ark as a god in itself rather than as a visual aid to draw their minds toward the invisible Creator. When the ark arrived at Israel's camp, a great triumphant shout rose from the soldiers. The Philistines, good scouts that they were, noted the whole thing and trembled, for they too viewed the ark as Israel's god, and a mighty one at that. They concluded if they were going down, it would be while fighting like warriors and they would make a battle of it.

But to everyone's surprise, Philistia included, Israel suffered an overwhelming defeat that day. And worst of all, the Philistines captured the ark of God.

A runner brought news of the disaster to Eli at Shiloh, whereupon the old man fell backward off his bench and died. His traumatized daughter-in-law chose this ignoble moment to give birth to a son whom she named Ichabod, "The glory has departed."[8]

In a series of little-noticed Bible references, God gives another history of Shiloh—the invisible history, describing Shiloh's fate in terms particularly relevant to ancient Israel.

Anyone remotely familiar with Old Testament history knows the pathos with which God called upon that nation to repent in order to avoid a calamitous end. With every tool of persuasion available to Him, God urged Israel to change directions. One illustration He used was the fate of Shiloh. "I will treat this temple as I treated Shiloh," He said of Jerusalem. "This temple shall be like Shiloh." Just go to Shiloh; see how desolate and uninhabited it is. I shall treat this place, Jerusalem, the hub of religious life in Israel, exactly as I treated her.[9]

But what actually happened there? The Psalmist describes, from the perspective of the invisible world concerning Shiloh, events that brought desolation upon that city:

> *When God heard this, He was furious, [a]nd greatly abhorred Israel, [s]o that He forsook the tabernacle of Shiloh, [t]he tent which He had placed among men.*[10]

---

[8] Samuel 4:21, NKJV, emphasis supplied.

[9] Jeremiah 7:12; 26:9.

[10] Psalm 78:59, 60, NKJV, emphasis supplied.

The people of Shiloh committed themselves irretrievably to ignore God's commands, and then the glory departed, exposing Israel to defeat before her enemies. The years rolled by and eventually Jerusalem itself fell by the same dynamics. (See Chapter 12.)

The Demoniacs of Gadara

Another interesting illustration of God's role in destruction occurs in the gospel story of the demoniacs of Gadara, whom we first met in Chapter 2. When Jesus cast a legion of evil spirits out of these men, the demons requested permission to enter some nearby swine. In a move perhaps designed to reveal the hearts of local residents, permission was granted. Only then could the demons destroy, as they panicked the swine and plunged them over a cliff.[11]

Here Deity only *allowed* a destructive act. The demons could not act out their destructive purposes without that permission. The attitude of local residents in response to this episode reflects economic rather than human concerns. The herdsmen of Gadara might have rejoiced at the deliverance of these unfortunate men, but they did not. Instead, responding to what they perceived as an economic threat, they put the blame on Jesus and cast their Savior out.

The Red Sea Crossing

The passage through the Red Sea—successfully by Israel, unsuccessfully by the Egyptians—can be described in terms of our alternate model of God's character, even though on the surface God appears indifferent to Egypt's fate.

First, we look for the Scriptural weight of evidence. The best example, the heaviest weight, is the example of the life of Jesus. We must bring God's character in the destruction of Pharaoh's army, into alignment with the character He displayed while He walked among men on earth.

The Red Sea passage becomes understandable if we place it in the setting of the great conflict between God and Satan. Did God have authority to suspend His natural laws on Egypt's behalf? No, but He did have this authority when it came to protecting Israel who still enjoyed the benefits of God's promises to Abraham, Isaac, and Jacob and who had

---

[11] See Mark 5, Matthew 8, Luke 8.

obeyed Him in the first Passover preparations. God gave Israel this rite, at least in part, as a way for them to demonstrate faith. When they obeyed by making the prescribed preparation, it gave Him jurisdiction to help them. These facts were probably lost on Israel, yet they obeyed nonetheless. It appears that even some of the Egyptians joined them in obedience, throwing in their fate with that of the Israelites.

In the history of the Exodus Israel did not violate God's directions as did the Egyptians under Pharaoh. The laws of the great conflict held sway. Having cast off every God-given opportunity to repent, Egypt under Pharaoh succumbed fully to the destroyer's jurisdiction. Satan stood at the head of Egypt's army, while God stood at the head of Israel. Once Israel reached the far shore of the Red Sea, God's authority to hold back the Sea ceased. Moses' holding his staff over the Sea signaled the end of God's jurisdiction. The miracle was not in releasing the Sea upon the Egyptians. The miracle was in holding it back for Israel. God did not here exercise His power to destroy the Egyptians but rather allowed natural law to return to its normal operations.

When these normal operations resumed and God acknowledged Satan's authority over the Egyptian army, the enemy could not protect his subjects from the laws of nature, nor did he likely want to, since God would ultimately get the blame anyway. In the natural, walking into the sea was suicide for Egyptians and Israelites alike. They had no reasonable expectation of living through the experience. God's saving the Israelites brought no guarantees to the Egyptians of similar favor.

The Fall of Jericho

A relative of mine shared this true story. A company of military recruits marched briskly and in cadence for miles during basic training at the time of the Korean War. As they came to a bridge the sergeant signaled a halt, and barked new orders. Stroll normally over the bridge, he said.

"Do not march in cadence, as it could collapse the bridge." Sound and movement create vibrations of air, earth, and everything around us. We have always known the capacity of the human voice, in the right conditions, to break glass placed a distance away from the sound. Could something similar have happened to Jericho?

Joshua 6 tells the story. Israel would march around the city in silence once each day for six days, with only the occasional sound of the trumpet's blast and the constant cadence of marching feet. But the seventh day they would march around the city seven times. At the end of the seventh day's seventh march around the city, the seven jubilee trumpets of the priests would sound a long, united blast, and the people would shout. The walls would then collapse to the ground. And so it happened.

Could the marching around Jericho have created movement deep within the earth that caused the ground to quake? Could the first six days have loosened the foundations of the city and the constant pressure exerted on the seventh day, with the added sound of the blasting trumpets accompanied by the great shout of the people have caused vibrations strong enough to make Jericho's walls collapse? We can't know for sure, but it is not wrong to look for alternative explanations when something appears to contradict what we know about God's character as revealed by His Son Jesus.

It appears the city had sinned away its guardian angels. What was Jericho's spiritual condition at this time? Had she sinned away her opportunity of grace? Everyone within the city had seen what Rahab saw and knew what she knew. She seems to have been a woman who did what she felt she had to do to assure survival for herself and her family. Yet she demonstrated sensitivity to divine influence and perceived that a divine power attended Israel, and the part of wisdom required her to align herself with that power. The entire idolatrous city could have saved itself by repentance and accepting the inevitable outcome of defeat as Rahab did, but arrogance blinded their eyes. They made the mistake of believing they held superior power.

"And the Lord said to Joshua: 'See! *I have given Jericho into your hand*, its king, and the mighty men of valor.'"[12] Just as Christ was *delivered up*, Jericho was *given over* to destruction. God had pulled His protectors out, and Jericho fell an easy prey to Israel.

Jericho had every chance to save itself, as did Rahab, had it cooperated in an obvious work of the God of heaven. Its fate speaks to us today. All could be saved if they only saw the wisdom of God's ways and surrendered to them. Only by cooperating with His ways can the universe ever be made safe for future eternity.

The Parable of the Unforgiving Servant

In reference to this, another story Jesus told found in Matthew 18:21-35,

---

[12] Joshua 6:2, NKJV, emphasis supplied.

tells a story that through the years has filled the hearts of readers with terror and hopelessness.

> *[T]he kingdom of heaven may be compared to a king who wished to settle accounts with his slaves. When he had begun to settle them, one who owed him ten thousand talents was brought to him. But since he did not have the means to repay, his lord commanded him to be sold, along with his wife and children and all that he had, and repayment to be made.*
>
> *So the slave fell to the ground and prostrated himself before him, saying, 'Have patience with me and I will repay you everything.' And the lord of that slave felt compassion and released him and forgave him the debt.*
>
> *But that slave went out and found one of his fellow slaves who owed him a hundred denarii; and he seized him and began to choke him, saying, 'Pay back what you owe.' So his fellow slave fell to the ground and began to plead with him, saying, 'Have patience with me and I will repay you.'*
>
> *But he was unwilling and went and threw him in prison until he should pay back what was owed. So when his fellow slaves saw what had happened they were deeply grieved and came and reported to their lord all that had happened.*
>
> *Then summoning him, his lord said to him, "You wicked slave. I forgave you all that debt because you pleaded with me. Should you not also have mercy on your fellow slave, in the same way that I had mercy on you?"*
>
> *And his lord, moved with* anger, *handed him over to the torturers until he should repay all that was owed him.*
>
> *My heavenly Father will also do the same to you, if each of you does not forgive his brother from your heart.*[13]

As mentioned, throughout the years and centuries in which Christians have read this story, it has provoked much unnecessary terror in them. They read that our Father in heaven is like the king and will do to us exactly as this king did to his slave. No one wants to be treated in this way or, rather, in the way it appears that the king is treating his servants. The main servant or slave in this story failed to forgive as the king had forgiven him, so the king felt all he could do was to punish him or release

---

[13] WEB.

him to the consequences of his own choice. Therefore, he *released* or *handed the slave over* to the torturers.

Notice, *the king did not do the torturing.* He merely released him—handed him over to the torturers. This story follows and underscores the structure of what we are learning about God. He is polite, courteous, and ever-caring. Words cannot express how His heart of love grieves when we do not choose His ways (in this story, forgiveness), when we do not make a beautiful and comfortable place for Him in our midst.

We need have no fear of the "king" in this parable; rather, we need to fear the moment when the "king" ceases His protective duties, in deference to our free will. Turning this man "over to the torturers" represents when a grieving God courteously and respectfully steps aside and releases us to suffer the consequences of wherever our behavior takes us, whatever we have chosen to do outside His will. It is not about personal offense. God simply can't reach us any more. We no longer can hear His gentle Spirit calling us to Himself. Therefore, the only thing left is for us to be released to follow our own heart in defiance of His will.

Scripture calls this moment, among other things, "the wrath of God," because of its negative and permanent effects on our life. We need not fear "the king" in this parable. We need only fear our insistent desires that will compel "the king" to release us to our own choice.

Testimony of the Apostle Paul

When the apostle Paul took up the pen to write a formal treatise of the gospel, the product of this endeavor, the book of Romans, became the *first* printed in a series of apostolic letters in our Bibles. The *first* chapter in the book of Romans, that *first* book, is arguably the clearest statement in Scripture defining "the wrath of God," starting in verse 18. When we examine that first chapter of Romans, we find translated a significant Greek word—*paradidomi.*

The *New Strong's Exhaustive Concordance of the Bible* defines *paradidomi* as: "to surrender, i.e. yield up . . . deliver (up), give (over, up)." A parallel word from Hebrew, *gazar*, occurs in Isaiah 53:8 and means "to cut down or off . . ., to destroy . . . cut down (off)." Another Hebrew parallel, *arah*, occurs in Isaiah 53:12 and means, "to be . . . bare, hence to empty, pour out . . . leave destitute . . . pour (out)."

It seems that when Paul wished to define the gospel, he began by first defining the wrath of God, which, according to him, means that God

94

"*paradidomi*" or "gave (the wicked) up" or "gave them over" to the natural results of the ways of sin, which they preferred to Him. He says, "The *wrath of God*[14] is revealed from heaven against all ungodliness and unrighteousness of men, who suppress [hold] the truth in unrighteousness." He continues that when men and women choose the ways of sin, then God *gives them up* (v. 24) to their own ways. In verse 26 he repeats that God *gave them up* to their own sinful ways in which He could not participate, because they were repugnant to Him. God *gave them over* (v. 28) to whatever appealed to them more than Himself.

Our knowledge of the gospel begins with a knowledge of *paradidomi*. You may find in Paul's writings other comments that round out the role of *paradidomi* or the wrath of God in the gospel.[15]

Phrases to Watch For
Romans 1 is a key to our entry into exploring this beautiful message that God is love.

You will recall that Jesus, in the persona of sin, was "delivered up" for destruction. Some Bible translations say "handed over" rather than "delivered up." These and other phrases occur regularly in connection with statements of God's "wrath" or "anger." Watch for them. You may wish to begin your investigation with the book of Psalms in which this relationship particularly stands out.[16] Other phrases to watch for are "gave him/them over," "abandoned," "forsook/forsaken," "rejected," or that God "hid His face." Once you begin noticing them, you will find them everywhere in Scripture connected with those passages dealing with God's wrath.[17] They simply reveal that sin has caused the departure of God, meaning He is no longer free to protect individuals from the inevitable, terrible consequences of their rejection of Him.

No Darkness in God
The point is, when humans choose to ignore God to the extent they can no longer change their minds because they have destroyed their very capacity

---

[14] emphasis supplied.

[15] See Romans 4:25; 8:32, 1 Corinthians 5:5, 1 Timothy 20, 2 Timothy 2:17, 18, : 4:14-17, etc.

[16] See also Judges; 2 Chronicles 12-36, etc.

[17] Obviously, the fact that God "delivered" Daniel from the lions' den has a very different meaning from what we are talking about here.

95

to love the great Lover of our race, He will not—because he cannot—inflict Himself upon them against their will. If He did intervene in their life to protect them or help them in any way, that intervention would be inconsistent with the nature of love itself.

A typical statement covering this dynamic occurs in 2 Chronicles 15:2: "The Lord is with you while you are with Him. If you seek Him, He will be found by you; but if you forsake Him, He will forsake you."[18] The choice for separation is always, first, a human decision. But given this human decision, God then has no choice but to honor it. "My people would not heed My voice, and Israel would have none of Me. So I gave them over to their own stubborn heart, to walk in their own counsels." Rather than feeling glee at His chance now to "get back at them" for their rebellion, He says, "Oh, that My people would listen to Me, that Israel would walk in My ways! I would soon subdue their enemies, and turn My hand against their adversaries."[19] Only on the line between human free will and God's matchless, unconditional love could a picture such as this take place.

---

[18] NKJV.

[19] Psalm 81:11-14, NKJV.

7

Who Torched
Sodom And Gomorrah?

*"Ye know not what manner of
spirit ye are of." (Luke 9:55, KJV)*

T hen the lord rained brimstone and fire on Sodom and Gomorrah, from the Lord out of the heavens. So He overthrew those cities, all the plain, all the inhabitants of the cities, and what grew on the ground. But his [Lot's] wife looked back behind him, and she became a pillar of salt."[1]

Enough has been said by now that students of this topic could draw their own conclusions as to the way in which Sodom and Gomorrah met their end. However, some specific archeological and Biblical evidence exists regarding those cities, which supports our present thesis.

Until recently no evidence existed outside Scripture for the five Cities of the Plain involved in the story we call "Sodom and Gomorrah." For this reason many scholars questioned the story's authenticity, attributing it to Middle Eastern folklore. Those few who thought it might have some historical basis expected to find archeological evidence of this beneath the shallow southern end of the Dead Sea, basing their belief on the Scriptural description of the area as "the Valley of Siddim (that is, the Salt Sea)."[2] Israelis call the Dead Sea *Yam Hamaelach*, Salt Sea, to this day.

---

[1] Genesis 19:24-26, NKJV.

[2] Genesis 14:3, NKJV.

In the late 1970s however, the lowering of the Dead Sea's water level allowed excavation extensive enough to shatter this hope, since no trace of these or any cities could be found.

Meantime, some interesting things were happening in the area immediately east of the southern end of the Dead Sea. As early as 1924 the noted archeologist and scholar, William Foxwell Albright, and M. G. Kyle, president of Xenia Theological Seminary, excavated an elaborate place of worship there, which they termed *Bab edh-Dhra*. The site received little further attention until 1973, when other archaeologists discovered in the same area ruins of an ancient city, which they called *Numeira*. Interestingly, *Numeira* showed clear surface evidence of having been burned.

Although work continues, archaeologists now state that this area contains the ruins of exactly five cities, no more, no less, and that several display "spongy char," the residue of burning, so profusely one may scoop it up with the hand.

A Biblical Picture

Sodom and Gomorrah were very wicked cities. Ezekiel lists their offenses as "pride, fullness of food, and abundance of idleness" nor did they "strengthen the hand of the poor and needy."[3] The Genesis 19 story of Lot's protecting angels inside his home from fierce and ungodly men further underscores their vileness. In short, Sodom and Gomorrah were ripe for the wrath of God. And that wrath came, but how?

Sodom and Gomorrah Found?

Scripture describes the cities' location on the plain of Jordan as "well watered...like the Garden of the Lord, like the land of Egypt as you go toward Zoar."[4] You will remember that God spared the small city of Zoar at Lot's request that he be given asylum there.

Seeing this area today, one can scarcely believe it was ever so productive. Now a virtual wasteland, it fights the indigenous people who seek to wrest a livelihood from it. The writer of Genesis suggests that even in his time the land had changed dramatically, for in portraying the former productivity of this area, he says this was "before the Lord destroyed

---

[3] 16:49, NKJV.

[4] Genesis 13:10, NKJV.

Sodom and Gomorrah."[5] That terrible event apparently changed the character of the land down to our own time.

In contrast with the barrenness surrounding these sites, the countless streams feeding into the southeastern Dead Sea make the shoreline still very fertile, hinting that the rest of the land could have been equally productive at some time in the ancient past.

In 1980 the prestigious journal *Biblical Archeology Review* reported that Walter E. Rast of Valparaiso University, Valparaiso, Indiana, and R. Thomas Schaub of Indiana University of Pennsylvania, who were then excavating these five ruins, believed they had found the ancient Cities of the Plain.[6] Scripture further describes this area anciently: "Now the Valley of Siddim was full of asphalt ['bitumen,' RSV] pits,"[7] suggesting some type of igneous activity occurring within the earth's crust in that region. Today "the shores around the Dead Sea are covered with lava, sulfur, and rock salt. Gases escape from the surface of the water."[8]   Note the existence in this scenario of all the ingredients necessary to destroy these cities in a great fiery conflagration. Bitumen, asphalt, oil, gas—even salt to turn Lot's wife into a pillar. Another name for "brimstone," which Scripture says God "rained" upon these cities is sulfur, a major export of this region today. One need only consider the swiftness with which the ancient city of Pompeii met its doom via volcano to know something similar could have happened to these cities in such a volatile location.

Modern archeologists have concluded that a massive earthquake occurred in this region sometime in the ancient past which not only ruptured some of the cities and altered the landscape significantly, but also likely caused the sulphur, bitumen, and other lethal elements to explode high into the air and come back down burning with intense fire that rained on everything in sight. God did not personally hurl fireballs at Sodom and Gomorrah. Rather, He *did not prevent* this natural disaster, because the free-will choice of the people had denied authority for God to block this disaster from coming on them.

---

[5] Genesis 13:10, NKJV.

6 "Have Sodom and Gomorrah been found?", September/October, pp. 27-36; 300 Connecticut Avenue NW, Suite 300, Washington, D. C. 20008.

7 Genesis 14:10, NKJV.

8 *World Book Encyclopedia*, 1954, p. 1891. If you want to know more about this phenomenon do an Internet search for "Dead Sea" and "igneous".

The Great Rift

Stretching from the Dead Sea and Syria in the north to Mozambique in the south lies the earth's longest valley—the Great Rift. According to geologists, this interesting formation resulted from ground movement—an earthquake—along a major fault line at some time in the ancient past. *Encyclopedia Americana*, p. 351, says, "Outpourings of lava formed volcanic plateaus at places along the sides, as well as volcanoes in and near the valley."[9] Did these great volcanoes and this remarkable earthquake, destroy the cities of the plain when God no longer had authority to prevent such destruction?

The devastation of Sodom and Gomorrah created a legend for centuries. Like Shiloh, the fate of those cities became an object lesson to Israel.

How God Destroyed the Cities

> *Jerusalem stumbled, [a]nd Judah is fallen. . . . [T]hey declare their sin as Sodom; [t]hey do not hide it. Woe to their soul! For they have brought evil upon themselves.*[10]

> *The punishment of the iniquity of the daughter of my people [i]s greater than the punishment of the sin of Sodom, [w]hich was overthrown in a moment, [w]ith no hand to help her!*[11]

Most revealing, however, is a familiar reference often quoted to depict the pain God feels over the death of sinners:

> *How can I give you up, Ephraim? How can I hand you over, Israel? How can I make you like Admah? How can I set you like Zeboiim? My heart churns within Me. My sympathy is stirred.*[12]

God uses the name Ephraim as a generic term in the same way He sometimes uses the name Judah, to denote an entire population.

---

[9] "The Great Rift Valley." Danbury, Connecticut: Grolier, 1983, emphasis supplied.

[10] Isaiah 3:8, 9, NKJV.

[11] Lamentations 4:6, NKJV.

[12] Hosea 11:8, NKJV.

No other writer more poignantly portrays God's distress at the thought of *handing over* or *giving up* the nation to destruction. Scripture calls this God's 'strange act'—the act of releasing those He yearns to save even as He would one day *deliver up* the Sin-bearer in order to redeem an entire lost race. He compares such a prospect to the time He *gave up* and *handed over* Admah and Zeboiim.

Deuteronomy 29:23 and Genesis 10:19; 14:2, 8 give the names of all four cities destroyed when "the Lord rained" fire upon the Cities of the Plain: Sodom, Gomorrah, Admah, and Zeboiim. According to Hosea then, these last two cities, and by implication Sodom and Gomorrah with them, were *handed over* and *given up* to destruction. We now see that the potential for their fiery fate already existed within their environment. Unbeknownst to them and unappreciated, God and His agents had spent countless years protecting them from this very potential disaster.

This does not exhaust the Biblical evidence that God released these cities to destruction rather than personally executing that destruction. Deuteronomy 29:23-28 strongly supports the "Release" position:

> *[T]he coming generation of your children who rise up after you and the foreigner who comes from a far land would say, when they see the plagues of that land and the sickness which the Lord has laid on it: "The whole land is brimstone, salt, and burning; it is not sown, nor does it bear, nor does any grass grow there, like the overthrow of Sodom and Gomorrah, Admah, and Zeboiim, which the Lord overthrew in His anger and His wrath."*
>
> *Then men would say: "Because they have forsaken the covenant of the Lord God of their fathers, which He made with them when He brought them out of the land of Egypt; for they went and served other gods and worshiped them, gods that they did not know and that He had not given to them.*
>
> *"Then the anger of the Lord was aroused against this land, to bring on it every curse that is written in this book. And the Lord uprooted them from their land in anger, in wrath, and in great indignation, and cast them into another land, as it is this day."*[13]

Here the prophet draws upon the past to predict the future. At the time God communicated this to Israel through Moses, the story of Sodom and

---

[13] NKJV.

Gomorrah was an ancient legend at least four hundred years old. God wanted Israel to understand what would be the fate of their nation should they, like those cities, choose to separate from God through sin. It is a fact of history that the nation did apostatize. After many centuries defined by cycles of apostasy, subjugation to surrounding nations, repentance, restoration and again plunging back into the same gross sins that had characterized her before, she eventually succumbed to the army of King Nebuchadnezzar of Babylon who in 586 B.C. razed both the city of Jerusalem and the magnificent temple of Solomon within the city, killing or capturing most of the people and transporting many of them to Babylon.

But our text says there was to be something similar in the way God would destroy the Israelite nation and the way in which He destroyed Sodom and Gomorrah. It says people will be struck by that similarity, implying more than mere visual likeness. In fact, Israel did not experience the same kind of destruction from fire raining down out of heaven as did the Cities of the Plain. How, then, would Israel's destruction parallel the destruction of those cities? Did it mean that, in keeping with His courteous character, He reluctantly gave up the cities of Sodom and Gomorrah to the sin that they cherished instead of Himself and pulled His protectors out? Was He warning Israel of the same fate?

Israel did not remain loyal to God. She experienced all the adversity from which God tried to warn her. Since her fate corresponded with that of the Cities of the Plain, if we can discover God's role in the punishment of Israel, we may also come to discern the way in which He "rained brimstone and fire on Sodom and Gomorrah."

The Bible makes this revealing statement regarding the ignoble fate of this privileged and mighty nation at the hand of the king of Babylon:

> Zedekiah [Israel's king]...did what is displeasing to Yahweh his God. He did not listen humbly to the prophet Jeremiah, accredited by Yahweh himself. He also rebelled against King Nebuchadnezzar to whom he had sworn allegiance by God. He became stubborn and obstinately refused to return to Yahweh the God of Israel. Furthermore, all the heads of the priesthood, and the people too, added infidelity to infidelity, copying all the shameful practices of the nations and defiling the Temple that Yahweh had consecrated for himself in Jerusalem. Yahweh, the God of their ancestors, tirelessly sent them messenger after messenger, since he wished to spare his people and his house. But they ridiculed the messengers of God, they despised his words, they laughed at his prophets,

until at last the wrath *of Yahweh rose so high against his people that there was no further remedy.*

He summoned against them the king of the Chaldeans who put their young warriors to the sword within their sanctuary; he spared neither youth nor virgin, neither old man nor aged cripple; God handed them all over to him.[14]

How can I *give you up,* Ephraim? How can I *hand you over,* Israel? How can I make you *like* Admah? How can I set you *like* Zeboiim?[15]

Here, again, God depicts Himself as *doing* what He does not prevent. He "summoned" the disaster, "spared neither" youth nor aged. From the language used, one might think God Himself personally inflicted this disaster upon His people. But no. The prophet Isaiah says in crystal-clear language that God "removed the protection of [Israel and] Judah."[16] As in the case of His own Son, the Sin-bearer, He simply ceased to protect, and the result? release into the hands of destruction. Thus it was with Israel. And thus with Sodom.[17]

---

[14] 2 Chronicles 26:11-17, JB, emphasis supplied.

[15] Hosea 11:8, NKJV, emphasis supplied.

[16] Isaiah 22:8, NKJV.

[17] Contemporary accounts of archeological findings tend to support the conclusions of this chapter. To read current reports of what excavators have found and their conclusions regarding these findings consult a library or the Internet at such places as http://www.abu.nbca/ecm/topics//arch5.htm; http://news.bbc.co.uk/hi/english/world/middle/_east/newsid/_1497000/1497476.stm; http://www.biblearchaeology.org/post/2008/04/16/The-Discovery-of-the-Sin-Cities-of-Sodom-and-Gomorrah.aspx#Article, or do a search for other websites.

8

Those "Holy" Hebrew Wars

"Then Jesus said to him, 'Put your
sword in its place, for all
who take the sword will perish
by the sword.'" (Matthew 26:52, NKJV)

One of the endearing qualities of God's character is how He moves us gently from where we are and what we know, to where—with greater enlightenment—He wants us to be. No subject in Scripture illustrates this better than the violence and warfare of the Old Testament.

Abraham's War

Scripture records, as its first example of warfare, Abraham's military victory over the united kings of Mesopotamia, who had swooped down on the thriving cities of Sodom and Gomorrah and helped themselves to the resident's food supplies and other belongings and captured the inhabitants with his nephew Lot among them. We have no record that Abraham asked God what he should do in this instance. As far as we know he merely reacted; God was merciful and gave him a great victory.

At God's call Abraham and his family had moved to Haran from Ur of the Chaldees. We remember that this was the home of the Tower of Babel, and it was just a few generations after this structure was built and destroyed that Abraham was born. In fact, the five kings who unitedly threatened Sodom and Gomorrah originated in this same general area.

While archeology reveals their society as highly civilized, it is reasonable to suspect that they were thoroughly pagan as well.

Abraham at this time was still shaped to some degree by the cultural norms of Mesopotamian society, as we are influenced by ours. Cultural ways can be so pervasive within a civilization that those who have grown up with them seldom question what society in general has accepted as normal. We often don't notice a fact that stands out before us, because our minds are so steeped in society's ways that simply feel right and normal to us. You will remember that Abraham made many mistakes during his life span; i. e., the attempt to represent his wife Sarah as his sister through fear of the Egyptians. After that fiasco he tried something similar in Gerar. Then there was the Ishmael incident, where he bedded Sarah's servant to provide himself an heir. Finally God tested him on the top of Mount Moriah, telling Abraham to do the unthinkable—to slay Isaac with his own hand, and Abraham successfully passed this test of his commitment to and love for God. He simply did what God asked, believing that God could and would raise Isaac up again. At the end an angel caught his arm and prevented him from going through with this terrible act, no doubt originated among the pagans. The point is that faith grows as we grow and learn. Abraham had not yet fully cast off the influence of the plain of Shinar in his life. That may be what drove him to choose warfare when God could have remedied the problem in a better way. Yet our patient God did not condemn him for it nor did He tell him to do it. Abraham just didn't know any better.

Out of Egypt

The Bible next takes us through the experiences of the children of Israel as they transitioned from a life of slavery in Egypt to an independent nation. Tradition among the slaves held that soon would come release. According to a promise made long ago to their father Abraham by the God of heaven, they would serve a certain number of years in this foreign land and then depart with many possessions, and the time drew steadily to a close.

How could the Egyptians not know of the rumor, which passed quietly among the Hebrews and so energized them with hope? Pharaoh determined to quench it permanently by invoking the "ultimate solution" and commanded that all male babies be drowned in the Nile River. The escape of Moses from this trap must have seemed providential, particularly when Pharaoh's daughter spared his life and his own mother took up the task of providing his early education. In his youth he moved into the palace and commenced his education as a soldier in preparation to become a mighty military general.

The Hebrews, separate from yet a part of the Egyptian world, beheld all around them a mighty nation, made such through the strength of her military resources. Chariots, swords, horses and glittering garments of mail symbolized to these agrarian people the necessary trappings of power. Now here was their hero, Moses, in whom the nation's hopes lay, receiving as Pharaoh's grandson the highest military education available in the land. The timing seemed perfect.

One day, at least to all appearances, the time arrived. Moses, out for a visit among his people, spied an Egyptian mistreating a Hebrew slave. Recklessly, without thinking how it might affect his relationship with the Egyptian throne, he slew the ruffian slave-driver.

If he expected the Hebrews to thank him and rise up in revolution behind him, he overestimated their enthusiasm for freedom.[1] Next day he learned just how isolated he was from the affections of Egyptians and Hebrews alike and, exercising great prudence, fled as far from both as his sandals would carry him.

Nonmilitary Exodus
Had God wanted a military solution to the problem of Hebrew bondage, here was His chance. But their release was not to come in that way. Moses spent the next forty years in exile, herding sheep on the rolling slopes of Midian while getting to know the Lord in a way not possible amid the sophistication of an Egyptian palace. When pride finally surrendered fully to patience, when he had learned to walk with God in humility, when he had learned and accepted his own weakness, when he was practicing how to abide in Him, then God knew he was ready to lead *in God's way*.

It was then as he led the Hebrews out of Egypt that they never drew a sword. God merely set up a situation where proud Pharaoh had to make a choice, to yield to His sovereignty or harden his heart in rebellion. When Pharaoh led the nation in declaring that he "knew not God" and refused to comply with the instructions given through Moses, his free-will decision and that of his subjects pushed away God's protecting, sustaining presence from the nation, placing them squarely under the power of the destroyer.

---

[1] Acts 7:25.

Yet God's canopy remained over His own people. The battle was His and all the glory would remain His own.

Evidence indicates that God planned to take the children of Israel into the Promised Land exactly as He had brought them out of Egypt. "God did not lead them by way of the land of the Philistines, although that was nearer; for God thought, 'If the people face war, they may change their minds and return to Egypt.'" "The Lord your God, who goes before you, is the one who will fight for you, just as he did for you in Egypt before your very eyes."[2]

We have no record that the Israelites left Egypt equipped for war. Exodus 13:18 is the one text debated in this regard. This somewhat ambiguous text has been translated several ways in various Bibles, as follows (The portion of the text in question is underlined):

1. **King James Version:** "[T]he children of Israel went up harnessed out of the land of Egypt." *Ambiguous translation.*

2. **Amplified Version:** "[T]he Israelites went up marshaled [in ranks] out of the land of Egypt." *Placed, arranged, set up. Notice the nonmilitary spelling.*

3. **New American Standard Version:** "[A]nd the sons Israel went up in martial array from the land of Egypt." *Military translation*

4. **New International Version:** "The Israelites went up out of Egypt armed for battle." *Military translation*

5. **New Revised Standard Version:** "The Israelites went out of the land of Egypt prepared for battle." *Translated as war theme*

6. **Revised Standard Version:** "And the people of Israel went up out of the land of Egypt equipped for battle." *Military translation.*

7. **New King James Version:** "And the children of Israel went up in orderly ranks out of the land of Egypt." *Nonmilitary translation.*

---

[2] Exodus 13:17; Deuteronomy 1:30, NRSV, emphasis supplied.

8. Jerusalem Bible: "The sons of Israel went out from Egypt <u>fully armed</u>." *Armed for war.*

9. Complete Jewish Bible: "The people of Israel went up from the land of Egypt <u>fully armed</u>." *Armed for War.*

10. **Young's Literal Translation:** "<u>[B]y fifties</u> have the sons of Israel gone up from the land of Egypt." *Nonmilitary translation.*

Therefore, only the *King James Version*, the *New King James Version*, and *Young's Literal Translation* (and possibly the *Amplified*) seem to agree with me, that the Israelites did not leave Egypt equipped for war but rather they left in orderly ranks. This portion of Exodus 13:18 connects with a larger text (v. 17) that reads, in whole, "Then it came to pass, when Pharaoh had let the people go, that God did not lead them by way of the land of the Philistines, although that was near; for God said, '*Lest perhaps the people change their minds, when they see war*, and return to Egypt.' So God lead the people around by way of the wilderness of the Red Sea. And the children of Israel went up in orderly ranks out of the land of Egypt."[3]

It seems logical that if God took them the long way to the Promised Land to avoid war with the Philistines, He would not at the same time arm them for war.

Strong's Exhaustive Concordance
I do not find *Strong's Concordance* helpful in sorting out Exodus 13:18. It merely says that the word from which all those underlined words above have been translated is *châmûsh* in ancient Hebrew, which means in modern English, "staunch," which is further defined as "fifth." The various translators have given the text the meaning that made sense to them at the time. Assuming a need to arm the Israelites for battles on their way to the Promised Land, they felt that this text provided them the opportunity to imply that God did so. Yet the text clearly shows He did not want them engaging in warfare with the Philistines on a trail that would take them into the Promised Land and beyond. Then why would he approve of their engaging in warfare as they traveled the longer route?

---

[3] NKJV, emphasis supplied.

108

God did not send them out armed but merely provided direction so that they would go out in organized bands and not like startled chickens fleeing in all directions.

Bible Commentaries, however, do provide some insight. One states, based on the *King James Version* rendering, "that is, girded, equipped for a long journey. The margin renders it 'five in a rank,' meaning obviously five large divisions." It also refers to Psalms 105:37, which states they went out heavily laden with gold and silver; nothing about weapons.[4]

Scripture would appear to deny that they had weapons as they set out on this important journey to the Promised Land. Therefore, we now turn our attention to the question of their faith. We know that "without faith it is impossible to please him."[5] Hebrews 11:29 states, "*By faith* they passed through the Red Sea as though they were passing through dry land: and the Egyptians, when they attempted it, were drowned."[6]   Remember also that they had brushed lamb's blood on the doorposts of their homes and eaten the first Passover meal, as God instructed. In short, during this early phase they had faithfully carried out all the acts of trust in Him that the Lord had asked of them.

 But after they arrived on the far side of the Red Sea, something unexplainable happened. Their faith appears to have dissipated. Throughout Israel's history Scripture never again mentions that they, as a nation, ever showed faith. Some individuals had faith and God was surely faithful with them, but not the people as a nation. In fact, the same author who says that they walked through the Red Sea by faith states also that they "entered not in [to the Promised Land] because of unbelief" [lack of faith or trust in God].[7]

In the reference to "Jesus" in Hebrews 4:8, the literal translation is "Joshua," as it is translated into English. By mentioning Joshua it confirms that the writer is speaking about Israel as they entered Canaan. You will recall that this generation of Israelites died in the wilderness and it was their children who finally made it into Canaan. Now, Canaan is a type of heaven, and the entering into Canaan symbolizes

---

[4]*Commentary Critical and Explanatory on the Whole Bible,* prepared by Robert Jamieson, A. R. Fausset, and David Brown, 1871.

[5] Hebrews 11:6, KJV.

[6] NAS, emphasis supplied.

[7] Hebrews 4:6, KJV.

God's children entering into their heavenly reward. I get that. But still it cannot be denied that Israel had some degree of faith during that walk through the Sea but nearly no faith—actually, unbelief—afterward. What might have happened there on the banks of the Red Sea after their miraculous walk through it that totally changed their attitude toward God ever afterward?

It has been suggested that this change came about because they now gained access to weapons for the first time. When "Israel saw the Egyptians dead upon the sea shore"[8] they saw the Egyptians' weapons lying scattered all around them. Keep in mind that the entire Egyptian army had come out to retrieve their slaves. This was a huge army with lots of weapons. While the greater body of the Israelites danced, praised God and rejoiced over their victory, was another scene playing out apart from and unbeknownst to rejoicing Israel?

What am I proposing? "[A] mixed multitude went up also with" Israel out of Egypt.[9] This "mixed multitude" was composed largely of the offspring of Israelites who had intermarried with the Egyptians. Also it could have included mixed races of people from the lowest strata of society, slaves from surrounding nations who had been taken prisoner and pressed into labor, also Egyptians who felt it prudent to throw in their lot with the departing slaves, and so forth. This group "fell a lusting"[10] and largely influenced the Israelites to desire flesh to eat. The Lord agreed to send quail, although with disastrous results to the people. This loud minority greatly influenced Israel, and not for the good as they journeyed across the desert.

In short, although we are not told in so many words, it is reasonable to believe that the mixed multitude, as they stood on the shores of the Red Sea, saw and coveted the weapons that lay around the dead Egyptians' bodies. Did they ask God if they could use them? Or did they simply pick up the weapons, happy now that their own protection was in their own hands, and in doing so also influenced the great body of Israel to do the same? Their state of unbelief seems to have started here, according to Scripture.

Psalm 106:7, NRSV, emphasis supplied, provides additional support for this assertion. "Our ancestors, when they were in Egypt, did not consider

---

8 Exodus 14:30, KJV.
9 Exodus 12:38, KJV
10 Numbers 11:4, KJV.

your wonderful works; they did not remember the abundance of your steadfast love, but *rebelled* against the Most High *at the Red Sea."* Did you know that the Bible says they rebelled at the Red Sea? Can we determine exactly what they rebelled about or *when* they rebelled? Hebrews 11:29 says, "By faith the people passed through the Red Sea"; therefore, they couldn't have rebelled during that walk. If they rebelled at the Red Sea it must have been on the far shore, because they had faith during their journey through the sea.

When did they rebel? *What* did they rebel about? Was it about defending themselves with war weapons? If not, what?

I have looked at this text in the *King James Version, the New King James Version*, and *Strong's Concordance* and have concluded that this enigmatic little text may support our alternate view. You are welcome to examine it for yourself.

What Would God Do?

Did this event actually occur in sacred history? And if it did, why does Scripture not record it? What would have been God's response to His people's efforts at self-protection? Would God have abandoned them at this crucial point in their history? Does Scripture provide sufficient backing to support this premise, or is it merely speculation and wishful thinking?

We can find indications of what God's position would have been in their later history as a nation. Their attitude toward slavery, deeply ingrained in Israel's culture, provides our first example. Herein is a case where God did not protest against slavery. Yet in spite of that, His faithful children throughout the years, though they could not discern it at first, have believed that to God this practice was grievous. The case against slavery rests upon God's commitment to the freedom and free will of His creatures, yet Christians couldn't accept it for centuries because on the surface Scripture does not condemn slavery.

William Wilberforce

In the eighteenth century at the height of the slave trade to Europe and the New World, William Wilberforce, member of England's Parliament, saw what most others could not see. An enormous portion of the world's economy at the time depended upon the trading ships that plied the seas with human cargo, destined for the slave auctions of the world. Virtually everyone in society, with the likely exception of the slaves themselves, had no problem with it. Scripture seems to accept this ancient practice. Many respectable members of society held slaves. The eyes of the world in general were blind to its barbarity. But Wilberforce had the vision and courage to condemn the holding of human chattel and devoted his life to stamping it out. This "David" took aim against society's "Goliath," threatening (they supposed) the world's economy, threatening slave-holders with performing their own manual labor. They might have to clean their own homes, work their own fields and bring in their own harvests. Slavery was institutionalized by this time, a fixture in the world, a monolith impervious to debate. But Wilberforce soldiered on.

In 1833, as this aged man lay on his death bed, word came that Parliament had at last passed a law outlawing slavery throughout the British Empire. America did not follow suit for another twenty-nine years. And contrary to expectations of the best minds of the day, the sky did not fall when truth triumphed and slavery ended throughout the land.

Wilberforce died three days after receiving the news. Somehow, where wrong was accepted without question, his eyes were opened to see it and to call sin by its right name. Today slavery is recognized for the abomination it is, even in the absence of direct censure of this practice in the word of God. Today we see it as self-evidently wrong. We wonder how anyone could ever have thought otherwise.

The Bible Record
How many examples can we find in Scripture where part of the story is missing or we must surmise from clues in other places in Scripture to get a fuller picture? Are there examples where man's insistence led God to defer, whether or not that deference resulted in good? For instance, we know that early on in the Bible record Abel brought to God a sacrifice that pleased him while Cain did not. God did nothing to Cain to justify his angry reaction. Presumably, the fire simply failed to descend on Cain's gift, showing God's nonacceptance. It has to be assumed that these young men already knew which gift would please God and which would not. Yet nothing is recorded in the story explaining when or what they were told. How did they know? We can only surmise.

Another instance occurred when Abraham hosted three visitors from heaven. When he learned that the angels' destination was Sodom where Lot resided and their purpose was to destroy the city, what did he do? He began to negotiate with God over the number of righteous men in Sodom that would prevent the intended destruction of the city. Amazingly, God yielded as Abraham talked out his terms.

And think of Ezekiel, who did not want to bake bread in the way God instructed him;[11] therefore, God relented and gave him other instructions for baking bread.

Likewise, Scripture does not condemn polygamy though God had made clear before the fall that His choice was one man and one woman to enter into the bonds of holy matrimony. Most advanced cultures today now recognize that fact.

The record shows how reasonable God is and how easy He is to deal with. He reserves His stronger warnings for preventing us from falling into the hands of the destroyer. Yet many times the Biblical record is incomplete or we have to research elsewhere in the inspired word until we find more information that completes the picture. Let me give one more example that tells us much about God.

Although God never intended Israel to have a visible king, He did not reject them when they demanded one. They longed to be *like* the nations surrounding them.[12] God warned them that they would come to regret this decision, yet He did not reject them for it. Instead, He yielded to their wishes and gave them a king as they insisted. With this example in mind we may ask, Did they early on desire to wage war "like" the Egyptians?

Comparing these examples, God's attitude toward taking human life also reveals relevant similarities. Slavery itself was wrong, yet God waited, still blessing His people while trying to make the practice easier on slaveholder and slave alike until more light could shine upon the people, and they would come to recognize the practice as abhorrent to Him. Thus we have God instructing the Hebrew people in proper ways to deal with slaves, yet never actually saying it was wrong, that they should not hold slaves. "[Y]ou may buy male and female slaves from among the nations that are round about you. You may also buy from among the strangers who sojourn with you and their families that are with you, who have been born in your land; and they may be your property. You may bequeath them to your sons after you, to inherit as a possession for ever; you may

---

[11] Ezekiel 4:12-15.

[12] 1 Samuel 8:5.

113

make slaves of them, but over your brethren the people of Israel you shall not rule, one over another, with harshness." "If a man lies with a woman who is a slave, betrothed to another man and not yet ransomed or given her freedom, an inquiry shall be held. They shall not be put to death, because she was not free; but he shall bring a guilt offering for himself to the Lord.[13]

The practice continued into the Christian era, for there we find Onesimus fleeing from his master Philemon and the apostle Paul writing to and counseling Philemon to take him back and be gentle in doing so, for Onesimus was now a brother in the faith. We now recognize the dreadful nature of slavery to the extent that most civilized societies turn their back on it. Could God also prefer that His children rest in His care and not attempt to protect themselves with human weapons of warfare? Might He prefer it without explicitly saying so? We have the example of slavery, polygamy, asking for a king and numerous other incidents in the sacred word that clearly leaves open this possibility.

War With Amalek

While this small work precludes our covering every instance of warfare in the Old Testament, it may be beneficial to critique at least an early example of Israel's going forth to battle. Otherwise, principles are provided which may be applied as you read about other military exploits of Israel.

The Amalekites traced their lineage back to Esau and were closely related to the Edomites. They came out to meet Israel at Rephidim in apparent cordiality. Then when the great mass of pilgrims had passed by, these villains fell in ambush upon the weary stragglers. Israel immediately mobilized for combat. Then, in one of the most noteworthy battles of the era, Moses, Aaron and Hur ascended a nearby hill. As the battle raged, Moses stood upon the hilltop with uplifted arms, his staff raised toward heaven. While he maintained this posture, Israel prevailed. But if he lowered the staff, Amalek triumphed. As the battle wore on, Moses could not maintain this winning position alone. Therefore, Aaron and Hur found a large stone, sat Moses on it and held up his arms until Amalek was vanquished.[14]

---

13 Leviticus 19:20-21, Amplified.

14 Exodus 17:8-16; Deuteronomy 25:17-19.

Israel's instant mobilization here suggests that the issue of how they were to defend themselves in event of enemy attack had already been discussed and settled. They evidently had weapons, though the Bible doesn't say where they got them. If God wanted to make a statement emphasizing their dependence upon His power rather than upon their military prowess, a stance that shows up repeatedly throughout Scripture, He couldn't have said it better than He said it here.

If they had shunned weapons and relied fully upon the care of God, how would they have handled Amalek's aggression? Would God have approved their lack of response to this crisis?

Who can say whether this crisis would have arisen at all had the nation internalized confidence that God is faithful and they would let Him take care of it. Whether they made a deliberate choice to take up the sword, or whether their persistent rebellion simply removed them from His authority, distrust obligated the nation to a whole different set of circumstances and experiences than they would have experienced under God's sole management. The decision to take up the sword may have been simply a further step in a series of rebellious choices, progressively removing them from under God's jurisdiction. Neither this incident nor any other combat situation in which Israel engaged was more threatening to them than the circumstances of their exit from Egypt, an event demanding a military solution—if there ever was one—from the human point of view.

God kept the events of their release from bondage continually before succeeding generations to emphasize His power to defend them with weapons to which they had no access. "If you should say in your heart, 'These nations are greater than I; how can I dispossess them?' You shall not be afraid of them, but well remember what the Lord your God did to Pharaoh and to all Egypt: the great trials which your eyes saw and the signs and the wonders and the mighty hand and the outstretched arm. . . . Moreover the Lord your God will send the hornet against them, until those who are left and hide themselves from you perish."[15]

Yet hornets, or the natural phenomena the hornets may have symbolized, were only one of God's many options for taking care of them. Scripture abounds with illustrations of the countless and effectual ways in which God can shelter those who put their entire trust in Him.

---

[15] Deuteronomy 7:17-20, NAS.

King Jehoshaphat

When Moab, Ammon, and Mount Seir came to war against good king Jehoshaphat, he might have trusted in the extensive fortifications built during his reign, but this he did not do. His method of dealing with this crisis contains all the Biblical elements of living by faith. He gathered the nation in a great prayer meeting. Lifting his voice to the God of might, he praised Him for past blessings acknowledging His position as head of the nation, claimed His ancient promises and then briefly described their present emergency. God communicated with a prophet on the spot, promising Jehoshaphat and his people that the battle was not theirs but His. On the basis of this promise, while it was still just a promise, the people claimed victory and went singing to the battle, armed alone with the mighty weapon of praise. "As they began to sing and praise, the Lord set ambushes against the men of Ammon and Moab and Mount Seir who were invading Judah, and they were defeated. The men of Ammon and Moab rose up against the men from Mount Seir to destroy and annihilate them. After they finished slaughtering the men from Seir, they helped to destroy one another."[16]

Their Protection Had Departed

Correctly understood, the Canaanite dispossession had nothing whatever to do with Hebrew military might. God had delayed the settlement of Abraham's descendants in the Promised Land until "the fourth generation," about four hundred years from Abraham's time, because "the iniquity of the" [Canaanites] was "not yet complete" in Abraham's day.[17] God would not encroach on Canaanite land on behalf of Israel while any hope remained that the indigenous people would turn to righteousness. The same rule existed for them as for all nations, for God "has made from one blood every nation of men to dwell on all the face of the earth and has determined their pre-appointed times and the boundaries of their habitation so that they should seek the Lord, in the hope that they might grope for Him and find Him . . . , for in Him we live and move and have our being."[18]

---

[16] 2 Chronicles 20:22, 23, NIV.

[17] Genesis 15:16, NAS.

[18] Acts 17:26-28, NKJV.

Faithful Caleb showed he understood this principle, for when Israel rebelled on the very borders of the Promised Land he said, "[D]o not rebel against the Lord, nor fear the people of the land. . . . *their protection has departed* from them, and the Lord is with us. Do not fear them."[19] Caleb recognized in the exodus the signal that these nations had sinned away their day of grace, that God could no longer reach them with salvation and that their final moral choice had removed them from God's authority and consequent protection.

Moses elaborates on this fact in Deuteronomy 9:1, 4, 5: "Hear, O Israel: You are to cross over the Jordan today, and go in to dispossess nations greater and mightier than yourself, cities great and fortified up to heaven. . . . Do not think in your heart, after the Lord your God has cast them out before you, saying 'Because of my righteousness the Lord has brought me in to possess this land.' . . . It is not because of your righteousness or the uprightness of your heart that you go in to possess their land, but because of the wickedness of these nations that the Lord your God drives them out from before you."[20]

Language of Violence

We would be remiss not to mention the terrible "killing" language that we often find in the Old Testament, including the directions of God to Israel to destroy the Canaanites. "[Y]ou shall conquer them and utterly destroy them"; "[Y]ou shall strike every male . . . with the edge of the sword. . . . [O]f the cities of these peoples which the Lord your God gives you as an inheritance, you shall let nothing that breathes remain alive, but you shall utterly destroy them."[21] If God's perfect will was something other than absolute destruction of the Canaanites by the sword of Israel, the language does not reveal it.

God invariably gives as a reason for the total annihilation of a people, "lest they teach you to do according to all their abominations which they have done for their gods and you sin against the Lord your God."[22]

---

[19] Numbers 14:9, NKJV, emphasis supplied.

[20] NKJV.

[21] Deuteronomy 7:2; 20:13, 16, 17, NAS.

[22] Deuteronomy 20:18, NKJV.

117

Placing this language within our new model, God may be saying here and in numerous other places as well, in essence: You have chosen to deal with this emergency militarily, in harmony with the methods of the nations around you instead of exercising the faith required to rely totally upon Me. Therefore, since you have chosen this method and I must either reject you for it or direct you in it, *I choose to do the latter*.

When you go to these nations to war, you must utterly destroy them; otherwise, they will be a snare to you for all future generations. If you're going to do it your way, He seems to say, then do it as effectively as would have been case had I simply let them go.

Here, as in their later decision to have a king, their choice is final. They came to regret their request for a king,[23] yet God neither reviewed nor revoked their servitude to one. Nor did He challenge their choice to be a military nation.

It is interesting to note, through the perspective of time, that even here, following what may well have been their own wayward choice, Israel proved unfaithful and ultimately reaped the predicted results of noncompliance with God's clear instructions. They failed to "utterly destroy" the Canaanites, who led them into idolatry and consequent separation from God from which the nation never fully recovered.

How might God have effected Israel's settlement in Canaan had they refused to use the sword? Without it, what chance did they have against the armies of Canaan? Yet God always has other options. He told the people repeatedly that He had no need of their swords[24] and He proved it many times throughout the Old Testament.

Jesus, the Model Man

Either Jesus expressed the character of God in every look and word and action—or He did not. If He compromised the truth one time, then we still look for Messiah. But I don't think we do. I believe Jesus was the real deal. If that be so, then the God-sponsored killing in the Old Testament requires serious reconsideration. This is particularly true in light of Jesus' statement,

---

[23] Scripture contains further evidence that in many cases God could not deal with Israel according to His perfect will. See for example Ezekiel 20:25 and Matthew 19:8.

[24] See for example Joshua 24:11, 12; Psalm 44:3; Ezekiel 33:26.

[I] t is these [the Old Testament Scriptures] that testify about Me."[25] "Put up again thy sword," Jesus said to Peter, "All they that take the sword shall perish with the sword."[26] At His mother's knee Jesus learned the eternal truths that He later taught during the years of His ministry. The Old Testament was His textbook. What did He learn from that source that shaped His own harmless character? He must have seen in those stories something that allowed Him in adulthood to counsel Peter, Don't take in your hands the weapons of war and violence.

Jesus was rejected because He didn't meet the definition of any messiah the people wished to welcome. The people didn't "get" His character, could not see their version of His Father in Him. He came to reveal His Father specifically because we did not understand Him. When Jesus told Phillip, "He who has seen Me has seen the Father,"[27] He identified Himself as the "base line" or standard of how to view God; therefore, the Old Testament must be reconciled to Him, not the other way around. Could it be that we still don't understand Him yet today?

To Recap
To recap, numerous Scriptural reasons exist to emphasize that God never intended Israel to defend themselves militarily, such as:

1. Jesus never confronted anyone with war weapons. In fact, He forbade it. Weight this point more heavily than all others combined.[28]

2. God did not intend for Israel to engage in war on her way to the Promised Land.[29]

3. Israel left Egypt unarmed.[30]

---

[25] John 5:39, NAS.

[26] Matthew 26:52, KJV.

[27] John 14:9, NKJV.

[28] See Matthew 5:43, 45; 26:52; Revelation 13:10, etc.

[29] See Exodus 13:17; Deuteronomy 1:30-32.

[30] Exodus 13:18.

4. God was in no way indebted to Israel's sword for their possession of the Promised Land.[31]

5. God gave them flawed instructions due to their hardness of heart.[32]

6. Victory always depended on their obedience to God, not on their military might.[33]

7. God intended to protect His people through the arsenal of nature, as He did in releasing them from Egyptian bondage.[34]

8. God did not allow David to fulfill his heart's desire of building the Sanctuary because he was a man of war and had shed blood.[35]

9. When Israel compromised by contracting multiple marriages, holding slaves and demanding a king, He did not reject them for it. Rather He tried to instill principles and requirements to make the best of a less than perfect situation, likely following the same procedure in regard to their choice to take up arms.[36]

Canaanites Rejected God's Ways

Through their commitment to rebellion against the principles of God's kingdom, the Canaanites rejected their only source of protection and life. Thus the record repeatedly declares that God "handed them over," "delivered them up," or "abandoned" them to the sword of Israel. But God declares, and their experience shows, that He was in no way beholden to Hebrew military power in order to bring about this outcome. The same principles functioned in the Canaanite dispossession

---

[31] See Psalms 44:3; Ezekiel 33:26; Deuteronomy 3:22.

[32] See Ezekiel 20:25; Matthew 5:21-48; 19:8.

[33] See Zechariah 4:6; 1 Kings 9:3-9.

[34] See Exodus 23:17-30.

[35] 1 Chronicles 28:3.

[36] See Exodus 21; 1 Samuel 8.

as have always existed where God's creatures have free will. Our patient God bears long, so very long, with human self-sufficiency and independence from Himself. In mercy He continues to provide for and protect humans who haven't the slightest awareness of their indebtedness to Him. But the time comes when their informed decision is final, their commitment to independence of Him unchangeable. Choosing to separate from Him, they become vulnerable to death, for their is no life apart from God.

9

The Case of Korah

[L]ove your enemies, bless those who curse you,
do good to those who hate you, and pray for
those who spitefully use you and persecute
you, that you may be sons of your Father
in heaven." (Matthew 5:44, NKJV)

Korah, Dathan, and Abiram, princes among the congregation of Israel, could not tolerate the present state of affairs in their (wandering) new nation. At Kadesh-barnea they had gotten to the door of their new country only to have Moses call them back again. He said their generation would spend forty years in the wilderness until they completely died off. Then their children would have the honor of entering the Promised Land, a prize they had once believed was theirs. Who does he think he is, they murmured.

Their leader, Moses, on the other hand, was unaware of the rebellion about to explode among the congregation until it happened. Korah, Dathan, Abiram and two hundred fifty of the princes of Israel had finally had enough.

> *You take too much upon yourselves [Moses and Aaron], for all the congregation is holy, every one of them, and the Lord is among them. Why then do you exalt yourselves above the congregation of the Lord?*[1]

---
[1]Numbers 16:3, NKJV, emphasis supplied.

The Rebellion in Heaven

In this confrontation between God's chosen leaders and the princes of Israel we see reflections of the first great rebellion in heaven, when Lucifer believed he could see what motivated Christ. He disdained the position heaven assigned to him—leader of the choirs of heaven, covering angel before the throne of God—and earnestly longed for the position of Christ, which he perceived as more favorable to achieving the exaltation for which his heart longed and and to which he believed he was entitled. He wanted so much to go up, to be exalted before his fellow angels, and he suspected Christ had entered into a conspiracy with the Father to deprive him of this role. He didn't say it aloud but he said in his heart, "I will ascend to heaven; I will raise my throne above the stars [angels] of God; I will sit on the mount of assembly on the heights of . . . [the north]; I will ascend to the tops of the clouds, I will make myself like the Most High."[2] This was his motivation; therefore, he attributed his own motivation to Christ Himself.

This psychological trait, projection, often renders individuals unable to discern a situation clearly through the pride that has blinded their eyes. Christ attempted to reason with Lucifer, to remind him that he could not create, could not give life to anyone or anything; therefore, his ambition could never be realized. Yet Lucifer clung to his desire to "ascend" much as Korah, Dathan, and Abiram dreamed of exalting themselves, while they accused God's appointed leaders of wanting this very same thing.

Did Christ wish to diminish Lucifer's ambition? Is ambition itself a bad thing? No. Not when it is properly motivated and has a worthy goal. But when it flows out of pride, when it seeks a selfish object, it unfortunately will not end well. And this fact Christ hoped to help Lucifer see, yet Lucifer continued his suspicions about the character of Christ, just as Korah and company eyed Moses and Aaron with suspicion.

Did Lucifer perceive Christ clearly? No. Scripture reveals that Christ's life was a study in constant "other-centeredness." "[T]he Son can do nothing of Himself, but what He sees the Father do; for whatever He does, the Son also does in like manner."[3] "For I have come down from heaven, not to do My own will, but the will of Him who sent Me."[4] He was

---

[2] Isaiah 14:13, 14, NRV.

[3] John 5:19, NKJV.

[4] John 6:38, NKJV.

steadfast in his subordination to the Father, faithfully seeking to magnify Him. He had no conspiracy with the Father. Philippians 2:5-8, arguably the best description of his nature in Scripture, says, "Let the same mind be in you that was in Christ Jesus, who, though he was in the form of God, did not regard equality with God as something to be exploited, but emptied himself, taking the form of a slave, being born in human likeness, [a]nd being found in human form, he humbled himself and became obedient to the point of death—even death on a cross."[5] Can you see that He came down? Jesus saw that the only true greatness is the greatness of humility. This is who He was and is. He had nothing to prove to anyone, thus He was free to minister to the needs of His fallen children. Lucifer couldn't see this through his pride. He continued to attribute false motives to Christ, much as Korah and friends now attributed false motives to Moses. Now let us return to the rebellion in the camp of Israel.

Israel's Rebellion

"You take too much upon yourselves [Moses and Aaron], for all the congregation is holy, every one of them, and the Lord is among them. Why then do you *exalt yourselves* above the congregation of the Lord?"[6] Hearing these charges Moses immediately fell on his face,[7] because He didn't see it coming, and His automatic response was to reach out to the Lord. Scripture says he was the most humble man on the earth.[8] Significantly, in that moment Moses and Aaron positioned themselves between the anger of the Lord and the congregation, praying, "O God, the God of the spirits of all flesh, shall one person sin and you become angry with the whole congregation?"[9] God expressed that He would eliminate the entire assembly and make Moses the new head of state. A similar event took place when Israel rebelled at Sinai's golden calf. That time Moses had said, "Yet now, if You will forgive their sin—but if not, I pray, blot me out of Your book which You have written."[10] Moses was willing to give up his own eternal life if Israel would thereby be saved. Yet Korah,

---

[5] emphasis supplied.

[6] Numbers 16:3, NKJV, emphasis supplied.

[7] Numbers 16:4.

[8] Numbers 12:3.

[9] Numbers 16:22, NRSV.

[10] Exodus 32:32, NKJV.

Dathan, and Abiram were unaware that each time this offer was presented to Moses, he deferred, stating he was concerned that it might make God look bad before the surrounding heathen. As Jesus after him, Moses was more concerned about God's image than about being leader of the nation.

Korah, Dathan, and Abiram

"You take too much upon yourselves, for all the congregation is holy, every one of them, and the Lord is among them. Why then do you *exalt yourselves* above the congregation of the Lord." Let us carefully evaluate that statement and the character of those who said it. Indeed the Lord was with them. But they seemed to have forgotten that when at Kadesh-barnea the ten scouts returned from reconnoitering Canaan, neither Korah, Dathan, nor Abiram spoke up. I don't remember hearing that their voices were raised in support of God's instructions to invade, as were Joshua's and Caleb's voices. Nothing was heard from these "great" men on that occasion. When the situation called for courage, they had nothing to give but cowardice. It was largely their own fault that, when they did not put their influence behind Caleb's and Joshua's position, they were turned back to the wilderness.

Yet when they were safely ensconced within their encampment, the whispering began. They blamed the leadership of Moses and Aaron for denying them the land that God had promised and instead consigning them to this place. They forgot that the Man in the cloud made the decisions. Moses and Aaron were only His agents in carrying them out.

Projection began, but they couldn't see it. They accused God's appointed leaders of "exalting themselves" and seeking their own glory. Since in projection accusers see in others the very traits internalized within themselves, we may be sure that they were projecting their own character traits onto Moses and Aaron. Korah, Dathan, Abiram, and their companions wished to be at the head of the congregation. They could not appreciate the humility of Moses nor see that the directions were coming from the Man in the cloud. It seems clear that Lucifer, insidious and cunning, was around, casting his baleful influence upon these men.

The Confrontation

As was his custom, Moses did not attempt to defend himself but deferred his defense to God. Jehovah was leader, a fact that the rebels overlooked but which remained constant with Moses; he never forgot it. Challenged to a showdown, Moses suggests that the principals stand before the tabernacle with censers in their hands and let God decide the issue. God then told Moses, "Tell everyone to stand away from the tents of Korah, Dathan, and Abiram." Moses so instructs the people.

"Then Moses said: 'By this you shall know that the Lord has sent me to do all these works, for I have not done them of my own will. If these men die naturally like all men, or if they are visited by the common fate of all men, then the Lord has not sent me. But if the Lord creates a new thing and the earth opens its mouth and swallows them up with all that belongs to them and they go down alive into the pit, then you will understand that these men have rejected the Lord.'

"Then it came to pass, as he finished speaking all these words, that the ground split apart under them. And the earth opened its mouth and swallowed them up, with their households and all the men with Korah, with all their goods. So they and all those with them went down alive into the pit; the earth closed over them, and they perished from among the congregation....And a fire came out *from the Lord* and consumed the two hundred and fifty men who were offering incense."[11]

Traditionally, we have taken this episode at face value. They rebelled. God, to maintain order and confirm the leadership of Moses and Aaron, split open the earth and destroyed the rebels. Then He finished off the two hundred fifty with fire.

Yet by now we should remember that in the invisible world, events may have occurred that are not described within this passage. "If the Lord creates a new thing . . . "[12] How might He create a "new thing"? *"He sees and describes Himself as doing what He does not prevent."* Does this event fall within that definition? Does He "create a new thing" by not preventing it?

If God released an earthquake all primed to happen beneath their feet at that exact moment, He could certainly have communicated that fact to Moses. Fire often accompanies earthquakes, as at Pompei, San Francisco, etc. Nothing in the description precludes our alternate view. But do we have any other Scriptural *support* for it in this matter?

---

[11] Numbers 16:28-35, NKJV, emphasis supplied.

[12] Numbers 16:30, NKJV, emphasis supplied.

The Counsel of Paul

Regarding Israel's exodus from Egypt, the apostle Paul counsels, "[D]o not become idolaters as were some of them. . . . Nor let us commit sexual immorality, as some of them did, and in one day twenty-three thousand fell; nor let us tempt Christ, as some of them also tempted, and were destroyed by serpents; nor murmur, as some of them also murmured, and were destroyed by *the* [definite article] *destroyer.*"[13]

The apostle does not intend to leave anyone out. In indexing the deaths on that long journey toward the Promised Land, they all fit in here somewhere. Note. . . .

"Do not become idolaters as were some of them (see Exodus 32). . . . Nor let us commit sexual immorality, as some of them did, and in one day twenty-three thousand fell (see Numbers 25:1-9); nor let us tempt Christ, as some of them also tempted, and were destroyed by serpents (see Numbers 21:6-9); nor murmur, as some of them also murmured, and were destroyed by the destroyer." And we know who he is.

The last entry of complainers, destroyed by the destroyer, includes the quail eaters (see Exodus 16; Numbers 11), the Kadesh-Barnea rebels (see Numbers 13, 14; Deuteronomy 1:19-46; 2:14-16); and Korah, Dathan and Abiram (see Numbers 16, 17).

Fire From the Lord

Further, Scripture goes on to say, "And a fire came out *from the Lord* and consumed the two hundred and fifty men who were offering incense"[14] Remember the story of Job, which says, "The fire *of God* fell from heaven and burned up the sheep and the servants."[15] Was the fire of God literally from God as the text states—or was it of Satan? We can expect fire from the sky to be unleashed in the future by demonic power.[16] It is not unusual for humans to speak from their own perceptions, nor is it unusual for demons to delight in causing God to get the blame for their evil interventions. Yet we know, because God has already told us in the oldest canonized Scripture story, not to be fooled by this. The fire coming down

---

[13] 1 Corinthians 10:7-10, NKJV, emphasis supplied.

[14] Numbers 16:35, NKJV, emphasis supplied.

[15] Job 1:16, NKJV, emphasis supplied.

[16] Revelation 13:13.

from the sky only *appeared* to come from God. Demonic power was clearly involved in the case of Job and likewise could just as easily have happened here. Aaron, at Moses' instruction, hurried to defuse the plague that started immediately afterward. According to the rules of the great conflict between God and Satan, until the people repented or atonement restored righteousness and God's protection, all the people remained vulnerable to the destroyer.

Mastema

Nor does this exhaust evidence that supports our thesis.

Moses' generation seems to have accepted that the Numbers 16 events occurred as written in the Old Testament. They may have viewed this strange (as we see it) presentation as merely a writing convention of the times and not questioned it at all, while it appears to our sensibilities that God is fierce and vengeful. We need only compare the Old Testament description of these events to the beautiful and perfect presentation of His Father's character that Christ gave us to see the problems the literal interpretation creates for us today.

Yet, historically, scholars have been aware of the problems created by this picture of God and some have attempted to explain them. By the time of the Christian era the apostle Paul clearly writes that this act of destruction was the act of *the destroyer*. Nor was Paul alone in his attempts to clarify.

The ancient Book of Jubilees, for example, offers some insights here. Written by an unknown author(s) not earlier than 160 B.C., this work traces the history of earth from Adam to the end of the world. While the Book of Jubilees is considered pseudepigrapha (of uncertain authenticity) by Protestants, Roman Catholics, and Eastern Orthodox Christians, it is accepted as canonical by the ancient Jewish community, and particularly by the Essenes who may have made it a center of their work. Either consciously or unconsciously the author(s) of this work helped to clarify the curiosity of the Korah, Dathan, and Abiram story that has caused so much confusion in the world and in the church.

The Book of Jubilees includes a character named Mastema, a demon who operates subordinate to the Father and does His "dirty work" for Him. This character is the mirror image of Satan, and operates identical to him. To illustrate, a quotation from the Book of Jubilees says this, regarding the exodus, "It was not God, but the arch-enemy Mastema who hardened the hearts of the Egyptians." We can see how he could also have been responsible for the deaths of Korah, Dathan, Abiram and the two hundred fifty leaders who perished with them in our story.

Other ancient sources share beliefs of pagan deities that bear a striking resemblance to what is described in this story. It was believed among the surrounding nations of that time that the god Mot was the god of death. This god was supposed to live under the surface of the earth but its jaws extended up to the surface of the ground and at times it would open them to ingest people to satisfy his hunger. With such beliefs all around them and having just come out of Egypt where such beliefs were common, it is clear that it would be to Satan's advantage, given opportunity by the withdrawal of God's protection, to reinforce such beliefs by supernaturally causing something like this to happen. Not only could Satan reinforce the notion that pagan gods really did have power to keep people in fear, but in this case he could deepen the suspicion that the true God likewise would act similarly to the pagan gods should people offend Him. And clearly that belief has persisted down through time to our day. Similar to our conclusions, both the apostle Paul and the writer(s) of the Book of Jubilees, along with a number of other ancient sources, provide evidence that acts of destruction can reasonably be attributed to someone other than Jehovah. Thus we find both the apostle Paul and other ancient author(s) creating a "passage" through which we can navigate in our efforts to improve our picture of God.

The Unforgivable Sin
This interpretation of the story of Korah, Dathan and Abiram generates more criticism than probably any other aspect of this new view of God. Critics say the destruction of Korah and his supporters was clearly a work of God, and those who believe otherwise are accused ironically of doing the devil's work in blaming the devil for this rebellion and its aftermath.(?) They wonder how it can be said that Satan destroyed these rebels, when God obviously executed their death sentence. To call a work of God a work of Satan constitutes the unforgivable sin, they say.

However, their argument is neither with me nor with this interpretation of the story; it is with the apostle Paul, who said that Korah, Dathan and Abiram were destroyed by "the" (definite article) destroyer. Consider these facts:

- This position is not *proved* solely with this incident; therefore, it cannot be *disproved* solely by attacking this one point. If the view is wrong, it must be disproved from A to Z, from Genesis to Revelation.

- If that cannot be done, it may be that God is sending advanced light to our world to facilitate our character development. If so, great caution should be exercised in interpreting it in order that either side may avoid committing the sin against the Holy Ghost.

- This incident could have happened either way—as traditionally believed or as described in *Light On the Dark Side of God*, if all we go by is evidence existing in the text. The context doesn't say that God split open the earth; it says only that He created a "new thing" and that "the earth" split open.

- Who put the envy into Korah's heart? Where did he get his insolent bold-ness to challenge the leadership of Moses and Aaron, two men whom God had ordained? Was this not clearly a work of Satan as reflected in the character of Lucifer? God's jurisdiction over them had been rejected. Therefore, He [God] could have nothing more to do with Korah, Dathan, Abiram and the two hundred fifty princes of Israel after they themselves committed to cherishing the spirit of rebellion.

Is it not interesting that Scriptural evidence exists that allows this incident to be described in terms of the alternate view? Satan, the first cause in any sinful program, whispered his own sentiments into rebel hearts and led them on until jurisdiction over their lives passed to him, and they were unaware that they had changed leaders. God was forced to withdraw, handing to the enemy authority over the rebels and their fami-lies, and thus they were "destroyed by the destroyer."

God merely lost authority to continue preventing their destruction. Physically He could have prevented it, but the exercise of the rebels' free will tied His hands. God told Moses what aspect of nature He had re-leased, as He told Satan in the story of Job. In both cases, God got the blame.[17]

---

[17] See Job 2:3, 5.

10

What Really Caused
Noah's Flood?

*"My Spirit shall not always strive with
man." (Genesis 6:3, NKJV)*

And God said to Noah, 'The end of all flesh has come before Me,
for the earth is filled with violence through them; and behold, I
will destroy them with the earth....

"'I Myself am bringing the flood of waters on the earth, to destroy from
under heaven all flesh in which is the breath of life; and everything that is
on the earth shall die.'"[1]

Thus begins a story familiar to anyone possessing the slightest
acquaintance with the Judeo-Christian tradition. Few legends of antiquity
provoke more controversy than the story of Noah and the flood. How
positive some sound when discussing the subjects of the flood of Noah's
day and how the world began. In their zeal, one would almost think them
eyewitnesses. While we do not know enough to be dogmatic about how
Noah's flood took place, we have enough information to make a good
case that it followed the same principles involved in other Biblical
examples of God's wrath, as described herein. Did potential for the flood
exist in the environment of antediluvian times?

Nothing in scientific fact refutes this Bible story (although "scientific"
philosophy may smile it to scorn). Individuals desiring further study will
wish to obtain John C. Whitcombe, Jr., and Henry M. Morris' *The Genesis
Flood*,[2] a standard work and comprehensive defense of the Bible story

---

[1] Genesis 6:13, 17, NKJV.

[2] Philadelphia: Presbyterian and Reformed Publishing Company.

of the flood based on recent scientific knowledge. Many other excellent materials are also becoming available today that defend the Genesis account of creation and the story of Noah's flood.[3]

The following account relates to the way in which a flood such as Genesis describes could have occurred. Did God personally drown the antediluvians, or did they "run Him off" through sin, depriving themselves of His protection, causing that great, worldwide flood?

Creation

In order to understand what may have taken place at the flood, we must first look at some of the details of creation.

On the second day, "God said, 'Let there be a firmament in the midst of the waters, and let it divide the waters from the waters.' Thus God made the firmament [the sky, where the birds fly], and divided the waters which were under the firmament from the waters which were above the firmament; and it was so."[4]

Modern readers of these words can become confused as to their meaning, for while they seem to describe recognizable conditions on our earth, they fail to correlate with anything we see above us today.

Yet Genesis insists that during creation week God "sandwiched" the sky (as we know it) between two great bodies of water—one on, in, and under the earth, and the other above that great heavenly expanse. Something upheld that canopy of water above the sky, screening the sun's harmful rays and diffusing light and warmth evenly upon the earth's surface, producing a "greenhouse effect," very unlike the one we read of in newspapers today. Evidently the dual powers of the pre-deluge sun and moon exerted drawing power on this canopy, much as the sun draws tons of water into the skies today by evaporation, forming clouds. "A mist went up from the earth and watered the whole face of the ground."[5] Water simply recycled in the area between these two great layers of water, much as it would in a terrarium.

---

[3] Macro-evolutionists charge Christianity with originating the idea of "intelligent design" as a euphemism for creationism; however, scientists with no particular religious bent, as well as those who are Christians, align themselves with intelligent design, because that's where the science lies. Other good resources that support Biblical creation and the story of Noah's flood are https://answersingenesis.org/the-flood/ and http://www.icr.org/creation-flood. These have not been questioned as to their belief in the present thesis; therefore, they are not endorsing it and are offered only for general background.

[4] Genesis 1:6,7, 20, NKJV.

[5] Genesis 2:6, NKJV.

The apostle Peter describes the old world as earth and sky, each in water and out of water, [6] an enigmatic statement indeed to try to match with today's conditions, yet matching perfectly with the description of earth as it emerged from the Creator's hand.

The obvious question at this point is: What happened to all that water *above* the earth?

The Sun and Moon

The Bible speaks of a time yet future when God will re-create our battered world. "[T]he light of the moon will be as the light of the sun, [a]nd the light of the sun will be sevenfold, [a]s the light of seven days, [i]n the day that the Lord binds up the bruise of His people [a]nd heals the stroke of their wound." [7]

In restoring the original creation, it appears that God will restore the moon's radiance until it is as the light of the sun. We may conclude from this that our moon was once a self-luminous body as bright as our present sun. Moon rocks gathered during space missions do not rule out their possible igneous origin.

Further, the light of the restored sun, much farther from the earth than the moon, will shine seven times brighter than now, suggesting that the pre-flood sun was seven times brighter than today.

It has been suggested that both moon and sun emitted exactly the right amount of heat in relation to their distance from the earth, the "vapor mantle," and each other to balance this great blanket of water above the antediluvian sky, in a constant stationary "orbit." This canopy, in turn, protected earth-life from the immense temperatures created by these giant generators, absorbing the heat evenly, and distributing just the right amount to maintain a perfect climate over the entire surface of the globe. Meantime down below, humans fortunate enough to live in this lush paradise, were taking it all for granted. Rather than thanking God for their wonderful blessings, they turned from Him in an orgy of self-centeredness. *The Genesis Flood* says this regarding the times: "The constant, almost monotonous repetition of [Biblical] phrases depicting the utter depravity of antediluvian humanity has filled the minds of believers with a

---

[6] 2 Peter 3:5.

[7] Isaiah 30:26, NKJV.

sense of awe and astonishment. Every statement seems calculated to impress upon its readers the idea of universal sin, not just the exceptional sins of this group or of that region, nor even of specific times or occasions, but rather the sins of an entire age and an entire race that had utterly corrupted its way upon the earth and was now ripe for the judgment of a holy God."[8] And judgment came, but how?

Grieving the Holy Spirit

In a statement that, until now, seemed strangely out of place in the Scriptural account of the flood, God says regarding this world of universal evil, "My Spirit shall not strive with man forever."[9] The apostle Peter adds that the Holy Spirit "preached" to disobedient "spirits in prison" (lost humans) while God waited patiently for Noah to complete the ark.[10] These and other references clarify the vital role of the Holy Spirit in antediluvian times.

Scripture depicts God not as an absentee landlord but as controlling and sustaining nature—as a present Power working in and through natural law to sustain, protect, and perpetuate life. Here in the world before the flood, the adversary had won virtually a complete victory. But the Spirit remained, supporting nature and speaking in His characteristic "still small voice" to the peoples' inner consciousness, "waiting patiently." As Noah's steady hammer blows drove nails into the ark, the Spirit drove a question into human minds. "I wonder if he's right?"

But the undercurrent of conviction gave way to conformity, for surface public opinion held Noah in contempt. When the ark was completed only eight people believed God sufficiently to enter. According to the "rules of the contest" and in harmony with His commitment to the free will of His creatures, God had no fair choice but to back off. The command went forth, "Release."

What happened next may not be fully known this side of eternity. Keep in mind, this work is not a scientific treatment of the subject. Rather, we are exploring whether the same principles operated at Noah's flood as at other events historically understood as "acts of God." We cannot conclude here; we can only theorize, just as macro-evolutionists theorize

---

[8] p. 18

[9] Genesis 6:3, NKJV

[10] 1 Peter 3:18-20, NKJV.

their models, because no one today was alive at that time to see what happened. Following are some ideas as to the way in which this disaster may have occurred.

Absent continued access to our Creator God, its energy Source, the moon ceased generating its own light, went out, becoming merely a reflector of the sun. For the same reason the sun diminished to its present intensity, upsetting the balance supporting the thick upper water mantle, and contrary to the best "scientific" projections of the day, rain poured down. Asteroid or meteorite activity may have played a part as well. The Bible also records a "breaking up" of the "great deep" at that time, suggesting great and powerful jets bursting forth from the waters on and under the earth's crust. Whether God's withdrawal precipitated each of these effects, or whether, domino-like, release of the water canopy, asteroids or meteorites initiated further disasters, which God did not prevent, we do not know. We do know that, due to the devastation and to atmospheric and other changes dating from this period, life on earth has not been the same since.

We also know that, following the flood, the saving of righteous Noah and his family tipped the scales back to God's side, giving Him authority to continue His rescue work for the human race. The earth was again, to a great degree, At-One with its Creator.

The Hovind Theory
Another compelling theory relies heavily on the idea that, early-on, a canopy of water surrounded our planet. Called the Hovind Theory after its main proponent, Kent Hovind, it suggests a comet could account for the dimming of the sun, the extinguishing of the moon, the damage to many planets in our own solar system as well as the annihilated lost planet astronomers calculate should be a part of our solar system. Where this planet should be circling the sun there is now only an asteroid belt, possibly the remains of the shattered planet. However, all this extraterrestrial damage may have absorbed the worst of the blow from the comet so that this world survived instead of being blown to pieces as was the other one. But enough of the comet struck this earth that it upset the delicate balance of the upper layer of water, causing it to condense and fall, along with the super-cold ice from the comet itself possibly adding much more water to this planet than was here originally at creation. This concept

has the support of a great deal of science and answers questions that other theories fail to address. Both ideas—original creation and the Hovind Theory—suggest that the flood resulted when the canopy took a major hit, and that became a leading cause for the flood water.

Jude gives a history of angels, assigned to maintain order throughout the universe, leaving their post of duty—going on strike, if you will—during the time of Lucifer's rebellion. In this idea, also part of the Hovind Theory, a huge comet could have careened toward the earth with no angels in place to control it. God, of course, knew all about it, but He was helpless to stop it in view of the great abundance of sin in the inhabitants of earth, rejecting the very grace that was protecting them. They had made their final choice. He now had no jurisdiction in the matter. He tried to warn them but they refused to listen. Finally, He told Noah, "Build a boat."

Science suggests that this huge comet (or asteroid or meteorite) moved through space at an incredible speed and greatly lowered temperature. The lowest our temperature gets on earth is about minus one hundred degrees Fahrenheit. Because outer space is very cold, this maverick comet boasted a temperature probably closer to minus three or four hundred degrees Fahrenheit. This huge comet exploded as it neared the earth, blasting debris out through space, causing pock marks on Mars, Mercury, the moon and other nearby heavenly bodies. The explosion ripped through the earth's canopy and destabilized its foundational structures, causing the rain to come down for the first time on earth.

The temperature of some of the falling frozen water at minus three or four hundred degrees resulted in the quick freezing of great mammoths and other animals with fresh food still in their mouths and undigested food in their stomachs. This would be physically impossible to occur at any temperatures higher than this. As a result of this massive infusion of cold temperatures on this planet, the earth responded with an the ice age. But, according to this theory, it came suddenly—not over a period of millions of years.[11]

The Testimony of Eliphaz
We can also find important clues in the book of Job to better understand

---

[11] Those wishing further information on the Hovind Theory may refer to:
https://www.youtube.com/watch?v=SY0rj-TEx4o. (Hovind's belief regarding the present theory is unknown.)

the flood. Five generations and perhaps around five hundred years from that event, its memory still influenced human thought to a great degree. The flood caused Nimrod,who lived about two generations from the flood, to build a great tower, and we suspect that one function of this great tower was to preserve lives in case of another flood.

Eliphaz, Bildad, and Zophar had the worldwide flood in mind when they came to "comfort" Job. Three times in the book of Job the King James Bible refers to flood waters, and the New King James translates "waters" to "flood" in Job 27:20.

In an interesting account from the book of Job, the protagonist quotes his wicked ancestors as saying to God, "Depart from us; for we desire not the knowledge of thy ways. What is the Almighty that we should serve him? and what profit should we have, if we pray unto him?"[12] Here the wicked are quoted as saying to God, "Depart from us." Can we bring this attitude any closer to the great flood of Noah?

Eliphaz asks, "Will you keep to the old way which wicked men have trod, who were cut down before their time, whose foundations were swept away *by a flood?* They said to God, 'Depart from us!' What can the Almighty do . . . ?"[13] This statement, along with several others from Job's "friends," suggest they, like the modern world in general, recognized the principle of human separation from God. But they, as we also so often do, failed to understand that when this alienation becomes incurable, God does in fact, pull back. Most importantly, He does not then return to execute revenge against His enemies for He doesn't have to do so. Without His protection humans are destroyed, one way or another. Job alone expressed an embryonic knowledge of this dynamic.

Some have expressed that Elihu's comments to Job and his friends represent the key to the meaning of the book. Certainly we need to study this book in depth, for the book of Job may afford fertile ground for future investigations relating to this topic. What is most important however, is that we begin to realize that there are viable alternative explanations for how the flood of Genesis could have occurred, whether it be the ones offered here or others, that harmonize much better with what is becoming

---

[12] Job 21:15, KJV.

[13] Job 22:15-17, KJV, emphasis supplied. Because the last two words are rendered differently from translation to translation, I usually leave them off; their presence or absence does not affect the meaning of the text..

clear about God's disposition and methods concerning the wicked who continually defy His authority and cast off His protection from around them.

Scripture promises a future when heaven's rescue work will end in victory and humans will enjoy a restored creation. The sun and moon figure heavily in those promises. Those bodies will return to their original intensity, and "Your sun shall no longer go down [diminish in power], nor shall your moon withdraw itself."[14] Yet "the Lord will be to you an everlasting light, and your God your glory."[15] No orb in the sky will engross the attention of the redeemed above the glory of their mighty Redeemer!

> "For a mere moment I have *forsaken* you,
> But with great mercy I will gather you.
> With a little *wrath I hid My face*
> from you for a moment;
> But with everlasting kindness
> I will have mercy on you,"
> Says the Lord, your Redeemer.
> "For this is *like* the *waters of Noah* to Me;
> For as I have sworn [t]hat the waters of *Noah*
> would no longer cover the earth,
> So have I sworn [t]hat I would
> not be *angry* with you."[16]

---

[14] Isaiah 60:20, NKJV.

[15] Isaiah 60:19, NKJV.

[16] Isaiah 54:7-9, NKJV, emphasis supplied.

11

Old Testament Types of God's Character

*"But Jesus withdrew with His disciples to
the sea." (Mark 3:7, NKJV)*

Throughout the Old Testament there are stories that illuminate God's character in some way and show his power to protect his people in surprising ways against enormous odds. It reveals His mercies which extend over all His creation—saved and unsaved alike—and shows in action the principles of the great conflict between earth and heaven. Here are just some of those stories.

Elisha, His Servant, and the Arameans
The king of Aram had a problem. He had declared war on Israel, but every time he planned to ambush Israel in a certain location, the king of Israel would never show up at that spot. "He [the king of Israel] guarded himself there, more than once or twice."[1] The king of Aram suspected an informer was somehow transferring intel to Israel. So he called his servants in and asked them, "Will you tell me which of us is for the king of Israel?"[2] One of his servants knew about the problem. The prophet Elisha received the information in a vision or dream and conveyed it to the king of Israel, he said. Immediately the king of Aram determined to go to Dothan where Elisha lived to take care of this pest who was ruining all his battle plans.

---

[1] 2 Kings 6:10, NAS.

[2] 2 Kings 6:11, NAS.

Elisha's servant went out in the morning and saw horses and chariots surrounding the city. Terrified, he called out, "Alas, my master, what shall we do?"[3] Elisha prayed, asking God to open the servant's eyes, and when He did the servant saw a great army of horses and chariots of fire around Elisha. When Aram's army approached closer to where Elisha and his servant stood, Elisha prayed again that God would strike them with blindness. And so He did.

The remainder of the story is a classic example of the message of God's character of love in action. Elisha and his servant took the blind army to Samaria, and when they were safely ensconced within the city's walls, he prayed again, this time that their eyes might see. Imagine the soldiers' surprise when they saw that they were outnumbered and helpless within Israel's grasp. Shall I kill them, asked the king of Israel?

No, said Elisha, I think we better feed them. So he had a great feast prepared for them and when they had eaten their fill he sent them back to their master in Aram. It must have impressed the king, because "[T]he marauding bands of Armeans did not come again into the land of Israel."[4]

Notice how prepared Elisha was for violent warfare. He had an encircling army of horses and chariots of fire to provide him ultimate protection. Could anyone have been more secure? Looking on that great celestial army Elisha could have reasonably concluded that God planned to engage in savage conflict against the Armeans. But no. Elisha executed His plan to feed them instead, and this plan, carried out, achieved Israel's goal of safety from the Arameans far better than warfare ever could have.

Jonathan and His Armorbearer

Saul was having a bad day. He faced the Philistine army of thirty thousand chariots, six thousand horsemen, and foot soldiers "as the sand which is on the seashore in multitude,"[5] estimated to be around one hundred thousand soldiers. His own troops hid in caves, thickets, rocks, holes, pits, and only six hundred soldiers remained in his army, although they were gripped with fear. Only two swords were available to Saul's army, while the Philistines were armed "to the teeth." Saul sat in the shade and wondered

---

[3] 2 Kings 6:15, NAS.

[4] 2 Kings 6:23 .

[5] 1 Samuel 13:5, NKJV.

what to do. Meantime, unbeknownst to Saul, his son, Jonathan, and Jonathan's armorbearer, caught up in the same situation, planned a bold move. Jonathan said, "[N]othing restrains the Lord from saving by many or by few."[6] They would go up to the Philistine garrison, and if the sentries said they would come down to them, then they would remain and fight in place. But if the sentries invited them up to engage the battle on Philistine turf, they would take that as a signal that the God of heaven would fight for them. And Jonathan was confident that the God of heaven would give them victory.

They went up, got the signal they wanted, and commenced the fight. They had slain about twenty soldiers when an earthquake took place under their feet. A great terror fell on the Philistine soldiers, disorienting them, "every man's sword was against his neighbor,"[7] and they proceeded to slaughter each other. The Philistines began fleeing in all directions. The Israelite troops, who had been so terrified before, emerged from their holes in the ground, picked up the Philistine weapons, and "followed hard after them."[8] And Israel enjoyed a great victory over the Philistines.

Did God require Jonathan and his armorbearer to slay anyone that day? Perhaps He needed some act of faith, as in Egypt He asked departing Israel to brush lamb's blood on the doorposts of their homes and requested that they walk through the Red Sea. But did He require killing humans as an act of faith? His subsequent sending of both an earthquake and a supernatural terror, was adequate to solve the problem. He never commanded them to kill nor so much as whispered to them that it would be a good idea to dispatch these Philistine troops immediately. Their culture blinded their eyes to the barbarity of their deed, and because they could not see it, Scripture says that God overlooked their times of ignorance[9] while they still grew in their knowledge of Him.

Azazel the Scapegoat[10]
Literacy was uncommon anciently and it should come as no surprise that

---

[6] 1 Samuel 14:6, NKJV.

[7] 1 Samuel 14:20, NKJV.

[8] 1 Samuel 14:22, NKJV.

[9] Acts 17:30.

[10] Leviticus 16.

the ancient Israelites were no exception. Because Israel left Egypt as a band of ex-slaves, near God's first order of business was setting up the beautiful Sanctuary and establishing symbolic rituals in connection with it to teach them how to worship Him and what was expected of them as they set out toward the Promised Land. Throughout their existence as a nation, except for one seventy-year period when they were subject to the Babylonians, its ceremonies were observed, teaching them the fundamentals of the gospel.

At the beginning of each year the festivals commenced. Passover was first; to remind them that they had been slaves in Egypt and how God had brought them out of that enslavement with a powerful hand. Fifty days following Passover was Pentecost, then trumpets, then the Day of Atonement. The last rite at the conclusion of the Day of Atonement, the last rite of their ceremonial year (except for Tabernacles, to celebrate victory), was a curious play in which Azazel, the scapegoat, played a key role.

It is interesting how Azazel became the scapegoat. Two similar goats were brought to the Sanctuary. Nothing distinguished these goats from each other. Lots were cast to see which would represent the Lord's goat to bring salvation and healing to the people. They sacrificed the Lord's goat and sprinkled its blood throughout the Sanctuary, representing heaven, on this important day. But Azazel, the scapegoat, the loser in the lot casting, was kept fastened *outside* the Sanctuary while its services went on, suggesting that nothing related to Azazel occurs in heaven, as the Sanctuary symbolized.[11] Azazel's role in the gospel story occurs solely on this earth. No blood was shed in the ritual involving Azazel. Unraveling the meaning of the scapegoat is a fascinating and informative exercise.

After the high priest completed services inside the Sanctuary, he came out and, with both hands placed on the head of the scapegoat, confessed the sins of the people over it. Just what is taking place here? What or who does Azazel represent? He has nothing to do with the Sanctuary. He functions solely outside it, meaning upon earth. He carries sin—all the sin of the faithful. Since it is a principle of Scripture that everyone bears the consequences of his or her own sin, this character must play a role in the sin of everyone since that is what is being confessed on him now.   Could

---

[11] Also the Sanctuary represents the hearts of God's people; therefore, if they are in right relationship to God's authority, Satan is limited to working only on the outside.

Azazel represent Satan? It was he who enticed the people into sin thus playing a part in that sin. It was he who tempted Adam and Eve and thus brought sin into the world in the first place. Although some might disagree, it seems reasonable to identify Azazel as Satan.

After putting the sins of the people on the head of Azazel, the high priest hands him over to a "fit man" who takes him far out into the wilderness. At this point the Jewish nation's depiction of Azazel breaks down. The instructions were that the fit man should release Azazel in the wilderness where he would have no further interaction with the people.[12] Israel eventually concluded the ceremonial year by casting Azazel over a cliff to his doom. Nevertheless, their original instructions were to *let him go* without violence.

The role of Azazel and the fact that he was simply released at the end of the ceremonial year in a place where he could never tempt or interact with humans again reveals much about God's plans at the end of time. God neither killed him nor had him killed. Nature alone could take the life of Azazel. What does that tell us about Satan in the last days? And what does it tell us about God?

The Plagues of Egypt

We know the story of the ten plagues of Egypt. We know that there will be seven plagues in the last days of earth.[13] What can we learn from the Egyptian plagues that will illuminate the plagues to come? We shall explore how they are alike and how different.

The Egyptian Plagues[14]

First Plague:	Water turned to blood
Second Plague:	Innumerable frogs
Third Plague:	Innumerable gnats or mosquitoes **Fourth**
Plague:	Innumerable flies (gadflies, *Amplified*)
Fifth Plague:	Death of livestock
Sixth Plague:	Boils on man and beast
Seventh Plague:	Hail, thunder, and lightning
Eighth Plague:	Locusts
Ninth Plague:	Darkness which was felt
Tenth Plague:	Death of the firstborn

---

[12] Leviticus 16:22.

[13] Some believe in adding the Trumpet's last three "woes" to the seven last plagues, in which case there will be *ten* last plagues, matching the type.

[14] See Exodus 7-11.

The End-time Plagues[15]

First Plague:	Foul and Loathsome Sores	→	**8ᵗʰTrp/Woe 1:** Do the locust
Second Plague:	Sea Turned to Blood		stings cause the sores?
Third Plague:	Springs & Rivers Become Blood		
Fourth Plague:	Sun Scorches People		
Fifth Plague:	Painful Darkness		
Sixth Plague:	Euphrates Dried Up	→	**9ᵗʰ Trp/Woe 2:** Euphrates
Seventh Plague:	Voice Says "It is done"	→	**10ᵗʰ Trp/Woe 3:** Voices in hvn

We notice some similarities in the plagues. Blood, for instance, appears in both lists. It was the first plague of Egypt and will be prominent in the end as both the second and third plague show bodies of water—the sea, the rivers, and springs— becoming blood. The ninth plague of Egypt and the fifth final plague involve a heavy darkness. Both lists came into being at similar times— the Egyptian list when Israeli slaves gained their freedom, and the end-times list when God's people finally gain their freedom from this world. Thus Egypt serves as a type of the end times.[16]

Notice, the Egyptian plagues were generally not lethal. The closest they came to taking the life of anyone was the fifth which destroyed the livestock. The seventh could have caused death only by ignoring God's warning to order the servants and the livestock inside as protection from the hail. Those who obeyed the Lord's warning lived. The people were made exceedingly uncomfortable by the plagues but nobody who respected God's warning and sheltered inside a building died. The same cannot be said for the tenth plague. We know that the tenth plague involved many deaths, and we have established that it was not God but Satan, the destroyer, who caused those deaths.

The same cannot be said for the plagues of the last days, when Scripture informs us that everyone will be vulnerable to death who lacks a certain seal in their forehead. What does the forehead represent? The forehead encases the frontal cortex, the area where thought and reasoning take place; it denotes *thinking*. Thinking a certain way. I will not say the RFID chip will not play a part but primarily it's how we think. And what we know. And how loyal we are to what we know and believe with all our heart. Everyone without this invisible seal is vulnerable to death. These plagues will result in the deaths of many in the last days.

---

[15] See Revelation 9, 11, 16.

[16]The plagues of Egypt seemed to have been chosen from the wide array of various gods they worshiped, as if to establish the superiority of the invisible God in heaven over the puny gods they had chosen to worship.

The primary difference between Egypt's plagues and the plagues of the last days is that the plagues of Egypt had the benefit of God's mercies. We don't usually think of the plagues in terms of mercies—how they represented God—, but when we consider how He warned the Egyptians, how patient He was, and that the people only experienced loss when they ignored His warnings, we witness a beneficent, merciful God. He released the power of plagues into the enemy's hands, one by one, and when Pharaoh agreed to let His people go, how quickly the plagues went away. We see God's hand of mercy everywhere in the Egyptian plagues.

That is not true of the end-time plagues. At that time earth people have experienced God's most powerful moves to save them. He has exhausted His arsenal of tools to heal their souls. Some have responded appropriately through surrender of their resistance to His love and have received His seal in their forehead. Some have not. But all have made a final choice. Thus God and His heavenly agencies are shut out of the lives of the lost because they no longer hear Him speaking to them. They have lost their capacity to hear His pleas of kindness.[17] His authority to protect them has passed out of His hands, and now with gut wrenching agony He must yield to Satan's demands that He remove Himself from their environs and hand them over to him.

But, true to His promise, He never leaves or forsakes those who are sealed, those who have committed themselves to Him and reveal their commitment by growing their character in harmony with the promptings of His Spirit in their heart. This group stands with mature characters in the likeness of Christ, fully reflecting their Savior, Christ Jesus.

The Fall of Babylon

Ancient Babylon, situated on the Euphrates river, reigned over the then-known world from about 626 BC to 539 BC. In its strength it conquered the world, but when it matured, it must have fallen deeply into the ways of sin. On the night Babylon fell the king hosted a great banquet in which the guests drank intoxicating spirits out of Sanctuary utensils that had been brought from Jerusalem when the Babylonians conquered Judea.

Fast forward to today. Genesis 11:9 says the word "Babylon" denotes confusion, the very word that describes our modern world. We tend to

---

[17] Romans 2:4.

think of modern Babylon as it functions in the spiritual world of Antichrist, the pope, the Vatican, the Roman Catholic hierarchy, and apostate Protestantism—and indeed it is.

But the Babylon of today encompasses the entire world. Besides confusion in the spiritual realm, there is confusion and pervasive deception in the world of education, of finance, of agriculture, of nearly everything that represents our modern society. Today the entire world is Babylon and it too will soon fall. Sin has cast its evil shadow everywhere, and as Isaiah 60:2 says, "[D]arkness . . . cover[s] the earth, and gross darkness the people." I believe Isaiah is referring to today, and Babylon today will fall by the same mechanism that caused the fall of ancient Babylon, who lost her Protector and didn't know it. Scripture says, "Your mother [Babylon] shall be put to great shame; she who bore you shall blush and be disgraced. Behold, she shall be at the rear of the nations [least of the nations]—a wilderness, waste, and desert. Because of the *wrath of the Lord* she shall not be inhabited but shall be wholly desolate."[18] She became so steeped in sin that she could not hear the voice of the Holy Spirit speaking gently to her inner being. It was not God's fault, but circumstances required that He stand down, withdrawing His protection. God's wrath fell on Babylon when His voice could no longer get through. Then the *paradidomi*—the handing over—occurred.

And the same mechanism that caused the fall of ancient Babylon will cause the fall of modern Babylon as well. Ancient Babylon fell when Cyrus diverted the Euphrates River making it possible for his troops to enter through the river bed under the city walls, exposing the weak point in their defenses and easily conquering the city. The "Euphrates" River is the focus of this prediction. In prophecy bodies of water represent "peoples, multitudes, nations, and tongues"[19]; these are the great multitudes of earth, the great populations; the masses. It was the failure of the body of water—the weak spot in their defenses— that made the conquering of ancient Babylon possible.

Modern Babylon will fall when the great populations of earth—the wicked whose majority opinion has placed them on the wrong side of history—suddenly realize that they have been deceived. Their eyes open, and everything will change.

---

[18] Jeremiah 50:12, 13, *Amplified*, emphasis supplied.

[19] Revelation 17:14, NKJV.

Gideon and His Band

What does the story of Gideon's victory over the Midianites tell us about the character of God? Gideon was the farthest thing from a hero. He trembled as he contemplated Israel's enemy, but the Lord directed him to action. He twice put out a fleece before the Lord in order to receive a sign, and God had answered in the affirmative both times. He was to lead Israel to victory over the Midianites and their sidekicks, the Amalekites. Still he trembled, for they vastly outnumbered his small army. Scripture says, "Now the Midianites and the Amalekites and all the sons of the east were lying in the valley as numerous as locusts; and their camels were without number, as numerous as the sand on the seashore."[20]

To make matters worse, the Lord had reduced the number of his small army from thirty-two thousand to three-hundred. Gideon was terrified, yet the Lord had promised that He would give this vast enemy army into his hands. He instructed Gideon to divide his army into three parts and surround the vast multitude in the enemy's camp. Each soldier had three "weapons" in his hands: a trumpet, a pitcher, and a torch inside the pitcher. They blew the trumpet, shouting, "A sword for the Lord and for Gideon,"[21] or "the sword of the Lord and of Gideon" as the authorized version gives it. Then they broke the pitchers.

What is the "sword of the Lord?" The trumpet sounds in the time of war to command the attention of the people; the last trumpet sounds for the same purpose when Christ returns. The light represents truth or what is needed to make right decisions, perhaps representing the Holy Spirit's influence. The pitcher is that which conceals the light of truth, and when it is broken and light streams out, the people know which way to go (or what decision to make). This is the kind of sword that God flourishes.[22] This is "the sword of the Lord." The Midianites and Amalekites could not run away fast enough. Surely it would be generations before they worked up enough courage to again threaten Israel.

But what about the killing that went on after the Midianites suffered that humiliating defeat before Gideon's band of three-hundred? Keep in mind that God never forces the conscience. Gideon's future ways were not

---

[20] Judges 7:12, NKJV

[21] Judges 7:20, NKJV.

[22] Hebrews 4:12.

pristine. He wandered a bit into the enemy's ways. Israel was so steeped in believing that righteous killing was not only acceptable but essential at times, and Gideon was a product of his culture. Did he arbitrarily make the decision on his own to go after the fleeing army, assuming that was what God wanted? I do not find where God ever commanded the killing to take place.

Other Old Testament Types

This does not exhaust the Old Testament types illuminating some aspect of God's character. See how many you can find.[23]

---

[2] See Chapter 8 for a thorough discussion of "killing" in the Old Testament.

12

What Is The End-time
Wrath Of God?

"He that leadeth into captivity shall go into captivity:
he that killeth with the sword must be killed with the sword.
Here is the patience and the faith of the saints."
(Revelation 13:10. KJV)

The difference in religions lies in the character of the one each calls "god." The doctrines and rituals of the church, which on the surface seem to define it, on closer view flow out of its picture of Deity. Our religious differences exist because we do not serve the same god. A mean-spirited, arbitrary god makes illogical demands on believers and relates to them in bewildering ways, sometimes driving them mad trying to "measure up." A reasonable, compassionate God makes sense; He exacts nothing from the believer; He simply reveals Himself, and that vision, that revelation of true beauty attracts the human heart to want to know and emulate Him.

The idea of "the wrath of God," so prominent in Scripture has lent itself through the centuries to a fearful picture of the Bible's God, with perhaps the most damaging charges centering on His end-time wrath, and since the warnings in Scripture against end-time wrath may have special meaning for us, it would be well for us to take a closer look at it.

Daniel and Revelation Speak

In the book of Revelation, references to final wrath occur thirteen times. A typical example reads, "If anyone worships the beast and his image, and receives his mark on his forehead or on his hand, he himself shall also drink of the wine of the wrath of God which is poured out full strength into the cup of His indignation."[1] Whatever God's end-time wrath is, it doesn't bode well for the sinner.

The book of Daniel also mentions "the wrath" in the same end-time context as Revelation.[2] It is an interesting exercise to read through the small book of Daniel and mark the statements mentioning "the end." Clearly, both the book of Daniel and the book of Revelation describe final wrath and address in particular those living in earth's last days. In that connection, Jesus predicted "wars and rumors of wars" as "the beginning of sorrows," "but the end is not yet.[3] No, but "when they say 'Peace and safety,' then sudden destruction comes upon them. . . . And they shall not escape."[4] Although "wrath" occurred from time to time throughout history, this coming era is called "the end," in recognition of the consequences of a final episode of "wrath" upon our planet. "At that time...there shall be a time of trouble, such as never was since there was a nation, even to that time."[5] "For then there shall be great tribulation, such as has not been since the beginning of the world until this time, no, nor ever shall be."[6] Revelation adds, "Then I heard a loud voice from the temple saying to the seven angels, 'Go and pour out the bowls of the wrath of God on the earth,"[7] an event signaling the start of the seven last plagues. In these bowls "the wrath of God is complete,"[8] indicating that Mercy can no longer block sin's natural consequences, for human free will has intentionally, knowingly, irreversibly accepted sin on a worldwide scale. "All the world marveled and followed the beast." "All who dwell on the earth will worship him,"[9] cherishing peer pressure and public opinion while despising the will of God clearly revealed in His word.

Regarding our day the apostle Paul says, "The coming of the lawless one is apparent in the working of Satan, who uses all power, signs, lying

---

[1] Revelation 14:9, 10, NKJV.

[2] For example, Daniel 8:19; 10:14;11:36.

[3] Matthew 24:6, 8.

[4] 1 Thessalonians 5:3, NKJV.

[5] Daniel 12:1, NKJV.

[6] Matthew 24:21.

[7] Revelation 16:1, NKJV.

[8] Revelation 15:1, NKJV.

[9] Revelation 13:3, 8, NKJV.

wonders, and every kind of wicked deception for those who are perishing, because they refused to love the truth and so be saved."[10] Where will our loyalty be found in that day? "The wrath of God" has a last-days application to which other episodes of "wrath" were but a prelude.

End-time Wrath

The Bible underscores the horror of final wrath with descriptions such as these: "Behold, the day of the Lord comes, cruel with both wrath and fierce anger, to lay the land desolate; and He will destroy its sinners from it. . . . Therefore I will shake the heavens, and the earth will move out of her place, in the wrath of the Lord of hosts and in the day of His fierce anger."[11]

On the surface, statements such as these appear to depict God as One who brings chaos, suffering, and pain into earth's environment at a magnitude which unfits it to sustain human life. Even the supremely compassionate and merciful Jesus warned of this coming "wrath." "He who believes in the Son has everlasting life; and he who does not believe in the Son shall not see life, but the wrath of God abides on him"[12]

After sacrificing His Son to give us hope, will God, in the final act, horribly torture and execute those who decline His generosity? How can this be? Are we obliged to approve in God that which we would condemn in humans? Again, given our traditional understanding of His wrath, we imagine a god who is both arbitrary and bloodthirsty, granting freedom of choice but intending to punish those who do not choose Him. This confuses us. It is no surprise that responses have ranged from universalism (the idea that these descriptions are all metaphors and all humans will at last be saved) to mind-numbing acceptance of all sorts of beliefs that don't make sense, to secularism and atheism.

Could it be that now, nearing our world's end, that God is sweeping away the fog in order that we might make our final choices based upon a clearer and more accurate appreciation of His character?

Although abundant Scriptural references exist which appear to designate God as the agent of wrath, at least as many references present Him in a very different way. First, the following examples almost objectify "wrath" as an entity having an existence of its own:

---

[10] 2 Thessalonians 2:10, NRSV.

[11] Isaiah 13:9, 13, NKJV.

[12] John 3:36, NKJV.

• [T]he Levites shall camp around the tabernacle of the Testimony, that there may be no *wrath* on the congregation of the children of Israel.[13]

• This we will do to them: we will let them live, lest *wrath* be upon us because of the oath which we swore to them.[14]

• Joab the son of Zeruiah began a census, but he did not finish, for *wrath* came upon Israel because of this census.[15]

• Whatever is commanded by the God of heaven, let it diligently be done for the house of the God of heaven. For why should there be *wrath* against the realm of the king and his sons?[16]

Is "wrath" a product of God's willful activity, or could it have an existence separate from Him, an existence where His character cannot be expressed?

Further, the emotion "wrath" or "anger" is not in the traditional sense an attribute of Deity. "[T]he works of the flesh are evident, which are: adultery, fornication, uncleanness, licentiousness, idolatry, sorcery, *hatred,* contentions, jealousies, *outbursts of wrath*, selfish ambitions, dissensions, heresies, envy, *murders,* drunkenness, revelries, and the like. . . . Those who practice such things will not inherit the kingdom of God."[17]

Finally, the Biblical picture of "wrath" would not be complete without noting a reference in the book of Revelation to the wrath of Satan.[18] Biblical evidence invites theologians to re-study this topic. As Christians we need to offer the world a better picture of the gospel than we have presented in the past, a picture that is both Scriptural and reasonable, a picture that sees sinners lose, while absolving God of any actions inconsistent with His character of love.

---

[13] Numbers 1:53, NKJV, emphasis supplied.

[14] Joshua 9:20, NKJV, emphasis supplied.

[15] 1 Chronicles 27:24, NKJV, emphasis supplied.

[16] Ezra 7:23, NKJV, emphasis supplied.

[17] Galatians 5:19-21, NKJV emphasis supplied.

[18] Revelation 12:12.

Biblical Types

With that background we are now ready to look for Biblical types that will help us understand God's role in final wrath. We have already explored some general principles. Can we find other helpful illustrations? Can we establish a connection between Biblical episodes of "wrath" and end-time "wrath?" Keep in mind the angel of Revelation who cries out, "If anyone worships the beast and his image, and receives his mark on his forehead or on his hand, he himself shall also drink of the wine of the wrath of God, which is poured out full strength into the cup of His indignation."[19]

Note the similarity with the following Old Testament quotation: "For thus says the Lord God of Israel to me: 'Take this wine cup of fury [wrath] from My hand, and cause all the nations to whom I send you to drink it. And they will drink and stagger and go mad because of the sword that I will send among them' Then I took the cup from the Lord's hand, and made all the nations drink, to whom the Lord had sent me."[20] To which nations did God send Jeremiah? He mentions several, but none possess as complete a Biblical history as the first mentioned. Therefore, we shall examine the fate of Jerusalem, a city which appears to have suffered "wrath" at two different times in her history.

Jeremiah 25 concerns the first episode in 586 B.C., already mentioned in connection with the destruction of Sodom. Here as in so many other places, the surface language suggests destruction through God's personal intervention. He will "bring evil" on the city.[21] He will bring Nebuchadnezzar of Babylon against the land.[22]

However, the context also reveals another dynamic operating in the destruction of Jerusalem anciently. God left His shelter as a lion leaves his "covert" or "lair."[23] [Psalm 76:2 says, "In Salem (Jerusalem) also is His tabernacle, and His dwelling place in Zion" (another name for Jerusalem).] He will "give those who are wicked to the sword."[24] When through sin the residents of Jerusalem rejected God's leadership, He had no choice but to

---

[19] Revelation 14:9, 10, NKJV.

[20] Jeremiah 25:15, NKJV.

[21] Jeremiah 25: 29, KJV.

[22] Jeremiah 25:9.

[23] Jeremiah 25:38.

[24] Jeremiah 25:38, NKJV.

depart; rather, to "stand down." And God's departure from the city exposed it to its enemy, Babylon.

Some seventy years after Nebuchadnezzar destroyed Jerusalem, Ezra the priest records a fact generally known among the Hebrews returning from captivity to rebuild the city. "Because our fathers provoked the God of heaven to wrath, He *gave them into* the hand of Nebuchadnezzar, king of Babylon."[25] Other texts as well indicate that the city fell, not because God personally brought it down, but because He was not there to uphold it. God did not choose this fate for Jerusalem; rather, the people chose to separate from Him and our gracious God deferred to their free will.

Jerusalem in 70 A.D.

Christians believe the kingdom of God suffered a major rejection in Jerusalem just a few short years before 70 AD. In the course of this rejection, note that the high priest Caiaphas *tore his robes*, which Jewish law from the beginning strictly forbade. "[H]e who is the high priest among his brethren . . . shall not uncover his head nor tear his clothes."

"And Moses said to Aaron [the high priest], and to Eleazar and Ithamar, his sons, 'Do not uncover your heads nor *tear your clothes*, lest you die, and wrath come upon all the people.'"[26] Caiaphas may have thought to signify his dismay at Christ's claim to Deity; however, long-standing Jewish tradition viewed the tearing of the high priest's garments as a symbol of separation from God.

Before Jesus ever embarked on His own ministry, his cousin John the Baptist warned the people to repent and flee from the "wrath to come." To what did the Baptist refer?

It is true, in a sense, that all the lost must face final wrath. "[T]he wicked . . . shall be brought forth [resurrected] to the day of wrath."[27] The apostle Paul says, "Jesus . . . delivers us [converts to His kingdom] from the wrath to come."[28]

But could John the Baptist have meant to warn the city to cherish her final opportunity for repentance through Jesus? Might he have had in

---

[25] Ezra 5:12, NKJ, emphasis supplied.

[26] Mark 14:63; Leviticus 21:10; 10:6, NKJV, emphasis supplied.

[27] Job 21:30, NKJV.

[28] 1 Thessalonians 1:10, NKJV.

mind the fast-approaching destruction of Jerusalem in 70 A.D. when he warned of "the wrath to come?" Significantly, in prophesying regarding the future destruction of Jerusalem, Jesus said, "[T]here will be great distress in the land, and wrath upon the people."[29] And the apostle Paul referred to the same event when he wrote to the believers in Thessalonica that the Jews had "filled up the measure of their sins; but *wrath* has come upon them to the uttermost."[30] Although about half a Biblical generation yet remained before Jerusalem experienced the horror and carnage of her final destruction, Paul could see the shadows gathering. It seems clear that the same factors which destroyed Jerusalem in 586 B.C. destroyed her again in 70 A.D.

God and Satan Collaborate?

Some challenge this view on the basis that God and Satan never collaborate. When God releases humans, some find it puzzling to understand how God induces the enemy at that exact moment, to do the destroying work. When considering this alternative concept of wrath, they seem to imagine God as whistling up the adversary to call his attention to the fact that here are some exposed humans for his lethal entertainment. He wants them destroyed, and now! The enemy then sashays over, surveys the situation, they negotiate a bit. Finally, at God's insistence, the enemy executes sentence upon the transgressor. But this is not at all what is being suggested here.

Imagine the wind blowing through a tree of very ripe apples. A stem snaps. What happens? Does gravity call to the apple to descend to earth? Do they spend time negotiating the details? No. Without a stem to hold it, the apple falls to earth. It cannot resist gravity in its own strength. It falls, because that's what apples with broken stems do.

Or imagine a sudden breach in a dam. What happens to the water? It flows through; natural law dictates the results of having a hole in a dam.

Similarly, the enemy is the destroyer. God is our hedge against him. When that hedge is breached for whatever reason, nothing then prevents Satan from exercising his character which is destructive. Will he always destroy when the hedge is breached? Yes, unless it is to his advantage to

---

[29] Luke 21:23, NKJV.

[30] 1 Thessalonians 2:16, NKJV, emphasis supplied.

delay awhile. This permits him to use his own agents as bait to induce others into sin. He seems to relish destroying, particularly when he can cast blame on God for it. But make no mistake about it: Sin in the life exposes humans to the destroyer. And Satan will, sooner or later, exercise his destructive nature against his servant, the sinner.

Great Past Civilizations

What of the great civilizations of the ancient past? Greece? Rome? A correlation has long been noted between the deteriorating morals of these great cultures and their final demise. Although we have no specific documentation supporting it, we cannot but wonder if the principles here set out were involved in bringing them down also. Could the era of history known as the French Revolution be described in similar terms?

Up to now it has seemed as if there were no accountability for what secularism, sin and man-made religion have done to the human race. Or, if accountability has seemed to exist at all, we thought God meted it out when He reached His "boiling point." But now it appears there is a fail-safe factor built into the very fabric of transgression itself that brings its own punishment. Sin separates from God, the only Life-giver and Life-sustainer in the universe, and consequences inevitably follow.

But who bears responsibility for those results—God or humans? We do not stay where the atmosphere is uncomfortable to us. God does, but only up to a point. When human free will pushes Him away forever, God reluctantly yet respectfully leaves. He has no other choice if He is to remain consistent with freedom, the principle necessary for love to exist at all in the universe. Legally He has no choice. Morally He has no choice. In His great conflict with the evil one, this is the law in operation. Humans use their own will to choose their own master. Otherwise, our ever-courteous God would take on the aspect of a bully, either forcing Himself into the company of those who despise Him, or altering His own character to accommodate wickedness, and that our changeless God can never do.

Yet before departing, He brings all the strength of His powers of persuasion to bear upon our hearts in attempts to convince you and me to live. "I have no pleasure in the death of the wicked, but that the wicked turn from his way and live. Turn, turn from your evil ways! For why should you die?"[31]

---

[31] Ezekiel 33:11, NKJV.

The very nature of human existence requires a Life-giver, not simply to initiate life but to sustain it as well. When God is denied authority to maintain that existence, when human free will obliges Him to depart for the final time, chaos and death inevitably result.

God, a Wimp?

There are those who do not wish to serve such a God as described in these pages. To them it appears that any god who refuses to do His own dirty work and personally torture the wicked with fire is a "wimp" and not worth serving. (Even though humans who do such things horrify us! By contrast, remember, Hitler at least killed his victims before burning them.) One man tells the story of Adolph Eichmann, who stared unrepentently into the very face of the hangman. The storyteller, an ethnic Jew, demanded the fulfillment of the "promise of hell," because he could think of no earthly punishment for Eichmann's crimes that adequately met his idea of the demands of justice. Somehow he felt that the "promise of hell" required God to personally administer that promise. In his and others' minds, only a willful act of punishment by a "sword wielding" God could accomplish the magnitude of suffering he had in mind for such fiends as Eichmann.

Those who harbor a desire for God to personally avenge their enemies unwittingly reveal their own characters. True, we are born with a natural inclination to seek vengeance when others do us wrong. But through the maturing process we should grow to understand there are better ways to deal with differences—that negotiation and wisdom can often avert the need for confrontation, that when all else fails the strategy of choice is to walk away. When individuals cannot appreciate the beauty of God's character in doing this very thing, it raises questions regarding their own maturity level. Maintaining a need to see God personally and willfully execute His enemies reveals a need for further growth in order to become Christ-like in character.

I do not mind serving a God who is gracious, loving, and intent on doing me good, as long as He is also a God who can do anything. "[I]s anything too hard for me?" He asks.[32] And when Sarah laughed at the thought that in her old age she would have a child, an Angel said to her,

---

[32] Jeremiah 32:27, NRSV.

"Is anything too hard for the Lord?"[33] Just look at the claim that Scripture makes for God. "Our God is in the heavens; he does whatever he pleases."[34] And what does He please to do? He pleases to care for me and you day and night. "In Him" our security is assured.

When God Leaves

The point which many find so hard to see is that when God departs, when people collectively push Him out, chaos ensues. When the lost are resurrected to judgment and find themselves separated from God, *there is nothing worse.* We cannot imagine in our wildest nightmares what will happen when the wicked realize they are lost—inexcusably and eternally lost. Words cannot convey it. Any punishment we might imagine for the devil himself could not reach the magnitude of the horror of that event, when "all nations drink of the wine of the wrath of God."[35]

But God Himself, who gave His Son to open a way of escape for us, will be ever free of any taint of culpability in the matter. It will be plain in the end that each individual will have made his/her own final choice. Free will is such a precious thing in His sight because it is the only way that love can thrive and flourish.

---

[33] Genesis 18:14, NKJV.

[34] Psalm 115:3, NRSV.

[35] Revelation 14:10, NKJV.

13

The Everlasting Burnings

*"Who among us shall dwell with the devouring fire? Who
among us shall dwell with everlasting burnings?"*
(Isaiah 33:14, NKJV)

Before ever sin appeared in this world, God warned Adam of the disastrous consequences of disconnecting from Him, earth's only Life-source, by indulging in sin. "Yahweh God commanded the man, saying, 'Of every tree of the garden you may freely eat; but of the tree of the knowledge of good and evil, you shall not eat of it; for in the day that you eat of it you will surely die.'"[1] Was God threatening His new creation that if they sinned He would have to kill them? Or was He warning of natural consequences so dire that at that point in time our first parents were incapable of understanding? God expected them simply to believe Him, and by obeying they would have protected themselves against the effects that sin would bring into their lives. Yet we know that both Adam and Eve used their God-given free will in an act of rebellion against Him; they chose to eat of the forbidden tree.

The serpent suggested God was extremely selfish and had not provided adequately for His children's needs. This contradicted God's gracious word to them, yet by accepting the enemy's position, they sided with the accuser that God could not be trusted. When distrust of God's word takes hold of the soul, it opens the door to disobedience. When we doubt God's love for us, it inevitably leads to fear, and we will feel compelled to look for alternate ways to provide for our needs outside of

---

[1] Genesis 2:16, 17, WEB, emphasis supplied.

159

God's generous provision. Virtually every sin springs from this fundamental fear that God cannot be trusted to care for us.

After our first parents sinned, the children of earth have been confused about what God meant by the warning He gave. The serpent may have reminded Adam and Eve that he and his demon spirits had sinned for a very long time and they still lived. No one had seen anything of the almost immediate death about which God spoke. Thus Satan raised doubts about God's integrity, and ever since the questions have lingered to haunt us. Clearly Adam and Eve lived many years beyond the day that they disbelieved God and sinned. So how can we trust a God whose words do not appear to ring true? God's credibility seems impossible to vindicate given this evidence.

This leads us to ask a most important question. Is death God's punishment for disobedience, or is there something far greater and more complex that our first parents didn't understand? God's trustworthiness was now on trial before the universe. What would God do with the remaining questions and confusion about His ways? Was Satan's position true, that God would not inconvenience Himself in any way to help His children? We now know that sin triggered a plan that had originated in the far reaches of eternity past, for Christ was "the Lamb slain from the foundation of the world."[2] The moment there was sin, already there was a Savior, holding this planet in place until earth's children understood and agreed that God's ways are just and true.

> *Great and marvelous are Your works,*
> *Lord God Almighty!*
> *Just and true are your ways, O*
> *King of the saints!*[3]

Fast forward four thousand years, and a voice is heard:

> *Behold, I come;*
> *In the scroll of the Book it is written of me. I*
> *delight to do Your will, O my God,*
> *And Your law is within my heart.*[4]

---

[2] Revelation 13:8, NKJV.

[3] Revelation 15:3, NKJV, emphasis supplied.

[4] Psalm 40:7, 8, NKJV.

Jesus, the Sacrifice For Sin

Before the universe and the entire human race God's Son, Jesus Christ, would come to this world and manifest His Father's character in fullness. Those persistent questions about God's trustworthiness and His character He would answer by living God's way in human form. On behalf of humans He would take upon Himself the full consequences of sin in order that they would understand what sin—living at variance with God's will—does. Before humanity He would reveal fully what are the wages of sin. The time had now arrived; God's Son, the "brightness of His [Father's] glory and the express image of His person"[5] would now walk among humanity.

Throughout His life Jesus magnified the Father by only reflecting His Father living in Him (by the Holy Spirit), just as humans were originally created to do.[6] He always did His Father's will[7] and thus revealed the gracious and merciful ways of the Father, proving that God could be trusted. And then He did what no one expected. He would be the first to experience the death about which God tried to warn Adam and Eve so long ago in a garden, even though He Himself had never sinned. Among earth's inhabitants He would be the first to experience second death. So we should not be surprised to learn that this event also transpired in a garden—the Garden of Gethsemane, extending out to encompass Golgotha and a lonely, borrowed tomb.

To understand the fate of the lost as demonstrated in the death of Jesus, we shall observe closely important clues seen in the experience of Jesus from the time He entered the Garden of Gethsemane until He died on Calvary. It was primarily during that time that "God made Him to be sin for us,"[8] and His death ultimately came about as a natural result of that "sinful" condition. At that time He typified humans who have made a final choice to turn from God's grace forever. Jesus took your death and mine, while those who do not choose to identify with Him in His conflict with Satan will experience their own totally unnecessary second death—a death they will prefer to what life would be under God's sole rule, a life in the atmosphere of love and complete vulnerability.

---

5 Hebrews 1:3, NKJV.

6 John 17:21.

7 John 5: 19.

8 2 Corinthians 5:21, NKJV.

Thoughtful observers conclude that the deaths should be equal. God the Father's role will be the same in both cases. In coming to understand the cause of the deaths of the wicked, keep in mind that Deity had nothing to do with originating sin; therefore, Deity should not be accused of imposing the consequences of sin. The similarity between Christ's death and the sinners' death went far beyond the Father's role, however. It is also seen in what Jesus experienced *emotionally* during this time, for He fully identified as one of us.

The Medical Literature

Jesus was the absolute revelation of the righteousness of God to His disciples, to His friends, and to everyone down through the ages. Yet from the time He entered the Garden of Gethsemane until His death on the cross, He felt that the onlooking universe—humans, angels, and demons—regarded Him as the absolute model of sinful rebellion against God. Although sinless still, He felt condemned as if He were guilty of earth's total sin burden, as the lost will carry their own sin burden when they have finally sinned away God's grace forever.[9] Let us observe Him now, from Gethsemane to the cross, so we may better understand the emotions lost humans will pass through on their way to final death in the end.

What caused Jesus' death? Was it the act of crucifixion itself? In spite of the shameful treatment He endured there, in spite of the pain of the crown of thorns pressed down upon His head and the whip lashed violently across His back, in spite of a world now steeped in belief that the cross caused His death, many are surprised to learn that He did not die from crucifixion. We will remember that in the Garden His "visage was marred more than any man, and His form more than the sons of men."[10]

Something was happening to Him *before* He faced the cross, something dark and horrifying, something that cannot be explained by mere knowledge of what the future held for Him. Attesting to the weight of darkness that saturated His soul, perspiration oozed from Him in great drops of blood that fell to the cold, dark earth. A search of medical literature demonstrates that such a condition, while admittedly rare, does occur in humans.

---

[9] 2 Corinthians 5:21.

[10] Isaiah 52: 14, NKJV.

Commonly referred to as hematidrosis or hemohidrosis,[11] this condition results in the excretion of blood or blood pigment in the sweat. Under conditions of great emotional stress, tiny capillaries in the sweat glands can rupture,[12] thus mixing blood with perspiration. This condition has been reported in extreme instances of stress.[13] During the waning years of the twentieth century, seventy-six cases of hematidrosis were studied and classified into categories according to causative factors: "Acute fear and intense mental contemplation were found to be the most frequent inciting causes"[14]

A more recent case is that of a young woman who presented to the medical staff, bleeding from her face and hands with no skin abrasions to explain why. "'There's no one explanation for the source of the bleeding,' the authors write." Others have hypothesized that capillary blood vessels feeding the sweat glands rupture, causing them to exude blood under conditions of extreme physical or emotional stress." Another team reported a similar finding in 2009 in the *Indian Journal of Dermatology*, citing six cases of prisoners facing execution and another case during the 1941 London Blitz."[15]

While the extent of blood loss generally is minimal, hematidrosis also results in the skin becoming extremely tender and fragile,[16] which would have caused Christ's pending physical insults to feel even more painful.[17] The condition behind such evidence is today called "acute stress cardiomyopathy" or "broken heart syndrome," a condition brought on by severe emotional trauma.

Jesus Died Voluntarily

While it is possible that humans could die this way from loss of blood, that is not what was occurring in this instance; Jesus was experiencing the complete process of giving Himself up to sense what the wicked will feel

---

[11] A. C. Allen, 1967, pp. 745-747.

[12] R. Lumpkin, 1978.

[13] See R. L. Sutton, Jr., 1956, pp. 1393-1394.

[14] J. E. Holoubek and A. B. Holoubek, 1996.

[15] *Canadian Medical Assn Journal.* 10/23/2017. Vol. 189, Issue 42.

[16] P. Barbet, 1953, pp. 74-75; R. Lumpkin, 1978.

[17] Dave Miller, Ph.D., *Did Jesus Sweat Blood?*

who reject God's love in the end. His death cannot be attributed to the cruelty He endured as our Substitute. Jesus said that He "lays down" His life, that He had the power in Him to lay it down and take it up again.[18] Mark, Luke, and John say that He "gave up the ghost."[19] Jesus Himself chose the moment when He would die, which coincided with the very moment of the evening Passover sacrifice.[20]

And as He did, He cried out with a loud voice, signifying that He still had vitality in His body. Normally a physically dying person's voice will fade out so at the end there is no strength left for a loud cry. When Jesus cried forth in this way, His words revealed the truth of His claim that He was laying down His life voluntarily, as He said, "Father, into thy hands I commend my spirit."

It was after this that a soldier drove a spear into Christ's side, and two distinct streams of water and blood flowed out, signifying that He died of *mental agony*—of a great and unbearable sorrow. This is the second of only two references to the literal blood of Jesus in the gospel accounts, and both of them combined reiterate the emotional cause of His death rather than any outside physical criteria. This is also why the writer John put so much emphasis on this event for he knew that understanding the truth about what actually happened on the cross was vital for appreciating the truth that Jesus came to reveal about His Father's character.

Christ's death occurred much sooner than anyone present expected. When soldiers went to break the legs of the men who were crucified that day in order that they could remove them from their crosses before the Sabbath, they discovered that Jesus had already died.[21]

When Joseph of Aramethea asked Pilate for Jesus' body, Pilate was astonished that He could be dead so soon; therefore, He sent a centurion to verify the death.[22] It was unheard of that someone crucified would die in such a short time. The briefest time known for crucifixion to cause death was two or three days, yet Christ died within six hours. Why? Clearly it was not the rigors of the cross that took His life but something else far

---

[18] John 10:15, 17, 18.

[19] Mark15:37, 29; Luke 23:46; John 19:30, KJV.

[20] Mark 15:33-37.

[21] John 19:32-33.

[22] Mark 15:43-45.

more powerful. And, remember, His death reflected the final deaths of the lost.

The Scriptures foretold the mental anguish that Christ would endure unto His death. "Innumerable evils" would compass Him, He said, and "therefore my heart [would] fail."[23]

"Reproach hath broken my heart; and I am full of heaviness; and I looked for some to take pity, but there was none; and for comforters, but I found none."[24]

Others in the past, in commenting upon Christ's death, attribute it to mental anguish as well and not to crucifixion. Geikie says, "The immediate cause of death appears, beyond question, to have been the rupture of His heart, brought about by mental agony."[25]

The Voluntary Sacrifice

Keep in mind, Jesus took it upon Himself to demonstrate the sinner's death before anyone else would be allowed to experience it. It was a death of mental agony, yes, but it was so much more. By observing it in detail we may get a better idea of what it involved.

"And the Light of Israel shall become a *fire* and His Holy One a flame."[26]

"Is it nothing to you, all you who pass by? Look around and see. Is any suffering like my suffering that was inflicted on me, that the Lord brought on me in the day of his fierce *anger*? From on high he sent *fire*, sent it down into my bones."[27] Notice, in these two Messianic prophecies that Christ's suffering is called a "fire." He uses the term "fire" symbolically, as a metaphor for the terrible sin burden He bore, for its affect upon His psyche. This "fire" the lost will also feel as they can no longer avoid considering their own sin when exposed by the great white throne judgment of Revelation 20.

---

[23] Psalm 40:12, NKJV.

[24] Psalm 69:20, 21, KJV.

[25] Cunningham Geikie, *The Life and Words of Christ*.

[26] Isaiah 10:17, *Amplified*, emphasis supplied.

[27] Lamentations 1:12, 13, NIV, emphasis supplied

All those that hate me love death.[28]

Are ye able to drink of the cup that I shall drink of?[29]

Jesus drank the cup of second death—a permanent death of the sinner's choosing; a death from which, by their own will and desire, there will be no awakening. An eternal death. A permanent death. All who have received Him will mortify the flesh and send it to second death in Jesus, who drank the cup for us. Those who cling to sin will choose to die the second death in themselves.

> Then said Jesus unto Peter, Put up thy sword into the sheath: the cup which my Father hath given me, shall I not drink it?[30]

Jesus would drink down that cup—and perish. The lost will drink it too.

> For as you drank on my holy mountain, [s]o shall all the nations drink continually; [y]es, they shall drink, and swallow, [a]nd they shall be as though they had never been.[31]

The wicked will drink this cup and go away to second death.

> Then death shall be chosen rather than life by all the residue of those who remain of this evil family, who remain in all the places where I have driven them, says the Lord of hosts.[32]

Comparing the experience of the lost to Christ's experience, do you get the impression that the lost will choose to go away to eternal death? The One who said, "I lay down My life that I may take it again. No one takes it

---

[28] Proverbs 8:36, NKJV.

[29] Matthew 20:22, KJV.

[30] John 18:11, KJV.

[31] Obadiah 16, NKJV.

[32] Jeremiah 8:3,NKJV.

[33] John 10:17, 18, NKJV.

from Me, but I lay it down of Myself. I have power to lay it down, and I have power to take it again,"[33] also said "Father, into thy hands I commend my spirit."[34] This denotes a giving up, a surrender, a submitting to the inevitable. Jesus experienced it. He even stated that this would happen. "No one takes . . . [My life] away from me, but I lay it down by myself."[35] This choice the lost will also ultimately make.

Judas, a Symbol of the Lost
Looking at it from the standpoint of the genuine sinner, Judas could not face his own life history after his exposure. He had planned ahead of time how his story would play out, but when he learned that it could never be that way and that he had not only failed to bring his own plans to fruition but had also betrayed the true Messiah to death, he no longer wanted to live; therefore, he went out and hanged himself.[36]

These two experiences—the death of Christ and the death of Judas— both give us vital insights into the final deaths of the lost.

Judas, as a type of the lost, chose suicide—a giving of self over to death in a very direct sense. Jesus chose to die also and even chose the moment He would die, though in His case it was not suicide but rather handing His spirit back to His Father. In the end the lost will see that life has nothing more to offer them, so they too will choose to go away from it altogether.

Duration of "Hell"
At this point, we should clear up a concept of punishment which has been a plague to the church of God and a stain upon the face of Christianity. How long will the wicked suffer the final judgment inflicted by sin? Most are familiar with texts that answer, "[T]hey will be tormented day and night forever and ever."[37] What does "forever" mean in Scripture? By now we should be getting used to going to Scripture for our spiritual definitions. The Bible contains a code that helps us understand what "forever" means in Scripture. We should not be surprised that it involves

---

[34] Luke 23:46, KJV.

[35] John 10:18, WEB.

[36] Matthew 27:3-5.

[37] Revelation 20:10, NKJV.

comparing one perspective with another perspective. Let us look, then, at the question of how long "hell" lasts.

> • Depart from Me, you cursed, into the everlasting fire prepared for the devil and his angels.[38]

> • [T]hey will be tormented day and night forever and ever.[39]

> • Its smoke shall ascend forever.[40]

We can see from this that Scripture frames the idea of final judgment in terms of everlasting fire, but what kind of fire is it? Is it literal or symbolic? What kind of torment is it? The pain of literal fire, or the agony of the symbolic fire that Jesus experienced when He died for us? In contrast, many references state that the wicked will one day be as though they had not been,[41] that they will one day be no more forever;[42] the wicked will be ashes;[43] the fire will devour or totally consume them,[44] and many more, thus...

How long will the wicked suffer final judgment?

One Perspective	Another Perspective
They will be tormented day and night forever and ever.[45]	The day which is coming shall burn them up ... they shall be ashes.[46]

---

[38] Matthew 25:41, NKJV.

[39] Revelation 20:10, NKJV.

[40] Isaiah 34:10, NKJV.

[41] Malachi 4:1; Ezekiel 28:18; Obadiah 16.

[42] Ezekiel 28:19.

[43] Malachi 4:3.

[44] Revelation 20:9.

[45] Rev. 20:10 NKJV.

[46] Malachi 4:1- 3.

The Bible record of Sodom and Gomorrah provides a key to this apparent contradiction. Remember, God warned His people through the prophets that they were repeating the history of those cities and would therefore share their fate, which turned out to be abandonment, when God lost authority to protect the cities. He also holds Sodom and Gomorrah up to us today as examples of the *duration* of that final fire.

How long did Sodom and Gomorrah burn?

One Perspective	Another Perspective
As Sodom and Gomorrah …are set forth as an example, suffering the vengeance of *eternal* fire.[47]	And turning the cities of Sodom and Gomorrah into *ashes*… making them an *ensample* unto those that after should live ungodly.[48]

If we had only these references, they would be enough, for look as we may we will find no cities of the Middle East burning since antiquity. The fire which consumed those cities obviously burned them up and died out ,[49] but why would Scripture describe them as burning eternally? And why would numerous Bible writers depict the final fire as "eternal," if it, in fact, burns out?

A final reference clarifies what "eternal" or "forever" can mean Biblically. "[A slave's] master shall also bring him to the … door … and he shall serve him *forever*."[50] That is "forever" to the slave. Only death can end forever. Only a world where death is unknown can enjoy a forever without end. To those unwise enough to take part in the final fire, forever or eternity ends for them at their last breath.

---

[47] Jude 7, NKJV, emphasis supplied.

[48] 2 Peter 2:6, NKJV, emphasis supplied.

[49] You will find this same pattern in connection with the "unquenchable" fire that destroyed Jerusalem anciently. (See Jeremiah 17:27 and 2 Chronicles 16:19-21) Unquenchable fire is simply fire which cannot be quenched by human effort.

[50] Exodus 21:6, NKJV, emphasis supplied.

.

John 3:16

For God so loved the world that He gave His only begotten Son,
that whoever believes in Him should not perish...[51]

Think about that word, "perish." In concluding that the fiery fate of the wicked burns on through eternity, have we considered the meaning of the word "perish"? There is no evidence in either Webster's Dictionary or in Scripture of the word "perish" meaning anything other than complete and final annihilation. Christ died in part as an illustration of how long the lost are engaged in the act of dying. Remember that He died from emotional torment much sooner than expected. Does this hint that the lost die quickly, as they process what has just occurred in their lives and give their lives over to death?

However, the word "forever" may be literal or symbolic scripturally, depending upon the context. We use the term "forever" symbolically to denote a seemingly unending period; for example, we might say, "I waited forever in line at the bank." Here context is king. Slavish holding to a literal interpretation when the context clearly calls for a symbolic one makes God appear arbitrary and inscrutable.

Another reason may exist for the sense of the everlasting so common in descriptions of that final fire—a reason which detracts not at all from the above logic. That is, when we understand the true nature and cause of the torment the lost will experience, that of resistance to the eternal, passionate, unquenchable love of God, then in reality the fire *is* everlasting and eternal while the suffering of the wicked is terminal and will not go on forever. The same fire that ever flows from God's throne is eternal because God is eternal. But the length of time that any being will resist love until they finally tire of fighting it and choose eternal death to escape will clearly be different, depending entirely on how much 'wrath' they have stored up within themselves during their lifetime of refusing to believe in and be transformed by the gracious love of God.[52] Clearly there will be differences in how long individuals will hold out in resistance to love before giving up, but sooner or later they will find eternal death the only viable option rather than living in the foreign atmosphere of heaven's

---

51 John 3:16, NKJV, emphasis supplied.

52 See Romans 2:4-5.

glory where nothing but selfless love is exchanged between those who dwell there.

But the real reason that fire is depicted as lasting forever or "everlasting" is that *its results will never be reversed through the ceaseless ages of eternity*, bringing it into alignment with these statements from the word of God:

- Never shalt thou be any more.[53]

- They will be as if they had never been.[54]

- They shall be ashes.[55]

Yes, hell has a terminus. That knowledge should come as a welcome spring breeze among earth's daily storms. But more, it serves as a backdrop for expanding our discussion about the deaths of the lost. It brings to us a greater realization of God's goodness and mercy. It removes Him, as we shall see, from all culpability in the deaths of the lost. It fulfills Bible prophecy.[56] It shows that the wicked suffer the results of their own choice—even their descent into eternal death.

God is a Sun and Shield
Fire exists in God's very presence. "A fiery stream issued and came out from before him."[57] That would be what the prophet Isaiah meant in Isaiah 33:14 by "everlasting burnings," for in verse 15 he goes on to identify the person who can stand in them as, "He who walks righteously, and speaks blamelessly; he who despises the gain of oppressions, who gestures with his hands, refusing to take a bribe, who stops his ears from hearing of blood, and shuts his eyes from looking at evil."[58] The "fiery stream" in which God dwells is a place of refuge for His children.

---

[53] Ezekiel 28:19, NKJV.

[54] Obadiah 16, NKJV.

[55] Malachi 4:3; Ezekiel 28:18.

[56] Revelation 18:1, Isaiah 60:1-3; Hosea 6:2, 3; Jeremiah 31:34; Habakkuk 2:14; Malachi 3:16-18.

[57] Daniel 7:10, WEB

[58] WEB.

Four young men stood in the midst of a "burning, fiery furnace" without harm, "and the form of the fourth is like the Son of God."[59] The burning bush is another example, where the bush did not consume, because God was in it. There were no fatalities at Mount Sinai either, caused by the fire of God that dwelt on the mountain top for so long. And the fatalities that did occur were at the instigation of the people. Clearly, there is a glorious fire in God's presence in which the righteous will dwell forever, unhurt and unafraid.

If the righteous flourish in the passionate fire of God's love, what happens to the lost—those out of harmony with God's ways—in this same scenario? Are they "zapped" and instantly destroyed by the sight of love in its purest form? Remember, God has nothing to give except love. Even though in keeping with His character of love He keeps them alive at this time, He has lost authority over this class of humans. Therefore, He can no longer impose Himself in their affairs. They are free to do what they want, but what do they want to do when they look on the King in His glory?

A Message From the Sanctuary

Back in Old Testament times the Israelites' Sanctuary worship service was a metaphor or play through which they could learn the outline and principles of the gospel. The Sanctuary told the story of human redemption. Everything was there—the sacrifice, the cleansing, the high priest, the blood, the light of seven candles, the bread of life, the altar of incense, and more—for their study and learning. However, the only fire was on the lampstand, symbolizing the constancy of the Holy Spirit's care; on the altar of incense, symbolizing the Christian's prayer life; and on the altar of burnt offerings, symbolizing the sacrificial death of Christ—and nowhere else. Nothing was burned alive in the Sanctuary services. However, in the surrounding nations' paganism that sometimes infiltrated into the worship service of Israel, the practice of burning children alive on super-heated idols was not uncommon. This was extremely abhorrent to God, and yet the message in these false worship practices has infiltrated Christianity, influencing opinions about both the cross of Christ and what will happen to the lost on Judgment Day.

What does the Sanctuary teach us about Christ's death? Did Christ experience actual fire when He died? If we had been there to see it, we

---

[59] Daniel 3:6-26, NKJV, emphasis supplied.

would have seen no literal fire involved in His crucifixion. Scripture says in the following Messianic text that Christ experienced fire. Yet the fire that He experienced was not literal but completely internal— in His thinking and emotions.

> *Is it nothing to all you who pass this way?*
> *Look and see if there is any pain like my pain*
> *Which was severely dealt out to me,*
> *Which the Lord inflicted on the day of His fierce anger.*
> *From on high He sent fire into my bones,*
> *And it prevailed . . .* [60]

Christ's death equals the death of lost humans, and fire will also one day be their lot. Scripture says, "[F]ire came down from heaven and devoured them."[61] It also talks about a "lake of fire" which is to be the final destination of the lost. Was it a literal, visible fire? Or was it an invisible, metaphoric fire that descended into Christ's mind and emotions, symbolizing the enormous inner conflict He experienced—while the fires lost humans experience will be literal? Some might insist so. But there is another alternative, one that is more consistent with what we have been learning about the kind of God Jesus came to reveal.

It makes more sense that, per Christ's example, a symbolic fire will be that which rages relentlessly inside their mind and heart as the lost process the full revelation of God's righteous character to the deepest reaches of their souls. Will they be thrown into a symbolic fire, the pain of which there are no words adequate to describe? a fire that no human can put out, similar to the death that Jesus died for their sins? What they experience is the power of their life-force exerting itself to live, yet conflicted upon seeing the Holy City in all its beauty and loveliness, longing to live there, yet painfully aware that they have totally unfitted themselves for life anywhere in the universe. They see clearly that rejoicing and praising the Lord is all that exists throughout God's creation, a lifestyle they have rejected and still reject. They know that they can't possibly live joyfully in it for they have lost all capacity for such joy and selfless love. This is the nature of that outer darkness, the place where there is weeping and gnashing of teeth of which Christ spoke.

---

[60] Lamentations 1:12, 13, NASV, emphasis supplied

[61] Revelation 20:9, NASV

173

The Interim

When Jesus comes to take His children home, there will be but two classes of people alive on the earth —the "saved" and the "not saved" or the lost. While descriptions of this event contain much information that is exciting and useful, suffice it to say that the saved will be taken to heaven to live with Jesus while the lost go to "sleep" for a thousand years. The apostle Paul wrote the best description of it.

> *But we do not want you to be uninformed, brethren, about those who are asleep [in death], so that you will not grieve as do the rest who have no hope. For if we believe that Jesus died and rose again, even so God will bring with Him [with Jesus, from the grave] those who have fallen asleep [died] in Jesus. For this we say to you by the word of the Lord, that we who are alive and remain until the coming of the Lord, will not precede those who have fallen asleep. For the Lord Himself will descend from heaven with a shout, with the voice of the archangel and with the trumpet of God, and the dead in Christ will rise first.*
>
> *["This is the first resurrection."[62]] Then we who are alive and remain will be caught up together with them in the clouds to meet the Lord in the air, and so we shall always be with the Lord. Therefore comfort one another with these words.[63]*

The apostle here seeks to calm early Christians who had recently experienced the death of a loved one. Having expected Jesus to return in their lifetime to take His children home with Him, they now wondered if these dear ones were to be lost forever because they had died the first death before Jesus returned. Was there no hope of eternal life for those who had died? The apostle hastens to remind the believers of Jesus' resurrection. In this letter the apostle assures them that the living righteous and the resurrected righteous will meet in the air to go home with the Lord together. Everyone else goes to sleep for a thousand years. You can read about this period in Revelation 20:1-6.

During this thousand-year time period there will not be one human left alive on this earth; therefore, earth now has sweet peace to rest from

---

[62] Revelation 20: 5

[63] 1 Thessalonians. 4:13-18, NASV, emphasis supplied.

humanity's destructive ways. Satan is alive and roams the land, but with no one now to tempt he has considerable time to think about the misery he has caused.[64] There is nothing in this picture so far to indicate the actual fate of the eternally lost.

At the end of the thousand years the lost are awakened (resurrected),[65] and with their awakening, Satan is free to deceive them once again. From this point we can consider more closely the subject of the final deaths of the lost.

The Final Judgment

The cross provided the scenario in which Christ died; however, He did not actually die from the effects of crucifixion. That was merely the surface activity that largely obscured his death's deeper aspects relevant to our present discussion. Christ was treated as sinful even though He was actually sinless; therefore, His behavior, while being treated as a sinner, we would expect to be different from the behavior of the genuinely sinful. Where Christ was meek, the lost will be angry; where Christ was forgiving, they will be filled with rage. Revelation 20 to 22 contains many references to the fate of the lost, but like other Bible doctrines, more information may be found throughout Scripture; i.e., Zechariah 14, Ezekiel 28, Isaiah 9:5, 18-21, etc.

The thousand years in heaven will have given the saved time to settle questions that may have troubled their minds about salvation and the fate of the lost, especially regarding God's role, His purposes, and how He has made His decisions. The final war upon the Holy City also serves as the ultimate demonstration of the incurability of sin in the hearts of the lost. God pays attention to detail; He leaves nothing to chance. So as He completes the great conflict, He will do so in such as way that it will win the minds and the everlasting loyalty of all His subjects with the unavoidable conviction that His ways are just and true.[66] "Affliction shall not rise up the second time."[67]

---

[64] See Revelation 20:1-3.

[65] Revelation 20:5

[66] See Revelation 20:7-15.

[67] Nahum 1:9, KJV.

At the end of the thousand years the lost will be awakened; they breathe again. The lost know not, however, that it was God, in keeping with His character of love, who has resurrected them. They only know that they are alive once again on Planet Earth.[68]

Meanwhile the holy city, New Jerusalem, like a bride floating down the aisle to meet her bridegroom, descends with all the furnishings of heaven, brilliant with the glory of God. The city is represented as a cube, as wide as it is long and high. It appears to have a wall around it with twelve gates made up of one huge pearl apiece; and underpinned with twelve foundations, each of a different precious gem. The splendor is so great that those recently resurrected outside the city can scarcely look upon it. Jesus descends, and as His feet touch the top of the Mount of Olives the mountain splits and becomes a vast plain where the city then settles down to the earth.[69]

The angels are there. God the Father, the Son and the Holy Spirit are there, all clothed in celestial fire, the symbol of God's great love. And, yes, those previously rescued at the second coming of Christ are there too, along with the saved of the ages, watching from the city's wall.

All humans who have ever lived are again alive, now together at the same time on Planet Earth. They wonder why everyone has been resurrected? What is the purpose of this event in their lives? God needs to allow Satan to finish developing his alternative kingdom to its full potential so that it can be clearly seen whether his claims against God can be proven to have any merit. Now, without any restraining influence of the Holy Spirit in the lives of those who have rejected God completely, Satan is given full reign to organize and synchronize his millions of followers to do whatever he desires. Can you imagine the vast hordes of humanity that include the great leaders of earth, famous military heroes, the scientists, the technocrats— still retaining the knowledge they took to the grave with them a thousand or more years before.

Using the mentioned references and a little sanctified imagination, we could visualize that a being of great splendor now appears before them. It is Lucifer, claiming to be the prince who insists he is the rightful owner of this world, and that the city they see rightfully belongs to him. Having no

---

[68] See John 5:28, 29.

[69] Zechariah 14:4

shield of conscience now to protect them from Satan's delusive sophistries and having been grafted into Satan's kingdom by their own choices, they readily become his deceived captives, eager to carry forward whatever deceptions he foists upon them.

To provide even more weight for his claims, Satan heals their maladies and sicknesses and makes the weak strong. Then as the crowning deception he tells them that it was he who resurrected them. A great shout of victory arises from the vast throngs. "Look at the relative size of our army compared with those in the city," their leader tells them. "We can easily overwhelm them."

They retool implements of war until they feel they are ready. Finally assembled into a great army, they march up to surround the holy city. The Bible says, "And they went up on the breadth of the earth and compassed the camp of the saints about, and the beloved city."[70]

> *When the kings joined forces, when they advanced together, They saw her and were astounded; they fled in terror. Trembling seized them there, pain like that of a woman in labor.*[71]

Arrested in the course of their march, they look up to see brilliant light flooding down on them from Christ sitting upon a great white throne high above the city, prepared for His final coronation. He has the record books of heaven with Him. "And I saw the dead, small and great, stand before God; and the books were opened."[72] A flood of revelation burns with exacting clarity into their psyche. As soon as these "books" are opened— the lost become fully undeceived.

Can you imagine, one minute thinking you served a being who could repair any defect in your body, who could raise you from the dead, who would let you go on sinning and give you eternal life anyway, and the next minute keenly aware that *you are lost with no one to blame but yourself?* Momentarily, a shock of fear paralyzes them. When those books are opened and the final judgment takes place, each sinner reviews his life and realizes that he is totally unfit to enjoy the atmosphere of heaven. He hears

---

70 Revelation 20:9, KJV.

71 Psalm 48:4-7, NIV.

72 Revelation 20:12, KJV.

the songs of the redeemed praising God in glory and knows that is the *only* sound that can be heard throughout the universe. At the same time he also knows that he can never find pleasure in that. Abruptly he wants to die because he knows now what eternal loss means.

"Weeping and Gnashing of Teeth"

Notice how Jesus speaks about Judgment Day using these words and phrases:

> ...throw him into the outer darkness; there will be weeping and gnashing of teeth.[73]

Judgment Day again:

> The wicked shall see it, and be grieved; he shall gnash with his teeth, and melt away; the desire of the wicked shall perish.[74]

> Let them vanish like water that flows away... Like a slug melting away as it moves along.... [75]

The glory of God's undiluted love now pours down upon them. They see that heaven is so near; it could have been theirs had they only allowed God's Spirit to repair their hearts in order that they could enjoy it, but now it is forever impossible for their character to change. Even so, their emotions burn within them with yearning desire for what God designed to give them in richest fulfillment, but they now realize that they are incapable of enjoying the only world that now exists. Seeing all this with precision, they abandon their leader who urges them to rush into battle with him. Now their loyalty turns to rage against him along with all those who helped deceive them during their life on earth. There is none left now to support him. He has been fully unmasked as the devil, the arch-rebel.

Everything is now out in the open, never again to be hidden, and God has been fully vindicated as righteous in every detail and without blame in all His dealings with everyone throughout history. With everything now

---

[73] Matthew 22:13, NRSV.

[74] Psalm 112:10, KJV.

[75] Psalm 58:2, 8, NIV.

clear and exposed by the full revelation of truth, the slander and lies that have fueled the rebellion are clearly exposed as a fraud, and those who have embraced them are now burning with the guilt of their sin and the losses they have incurred. This is the "outer darkness" with its "weeping and gnashing of teeth," of which Christ spoke. It is a psycho-emotional "unquenchable fire," the fire of God's great love pouring down around them while the internal fire of hopelessness drives them to realize that only death can release them from this supreme agony of spirit. This is the same burden of sin which led Christ to cry out from feelings of utter God abandonment just before He gave up His own life to the second death.

At this point the wicked turn with rage upon the now-debunked philosophies of Satan. Ezekiel 28 speaks of their "drawing swords against the beauty of his wisdom" and "defiling his brightness." Through metaphors Scripture depicts how they now realize the utter bankruptcy of Satan's system, which had promised them Utopia, yet they now see that the way of selfishness only results in complete ruin of their hopes and dreams.

The lost "shall throw you ...[Satan] down into the pit, [a]nd...[you will] die the death of the slain in the midst of the seas.... [They go down to oblivion, nevermore to be seen.] I destroyed you, O covering cherub, [f]rom the midst of the fiery stones...therefore, I brought fire from your midst , [i]t devoured you, and I turned you to ashes upon the earth [i]n the sight of all who saw you."[76] (Notice, Satan will be ashes) The lost now behold the full revelation of truth in the great conflict between God and Lucifer. Satan's lies, now forever fully unmasked, are destroyed, ruined, defeated. With no followers left he has no kingdom, no government, no societies to carry out his principles of action. He is thrown into the lake of fire, as his credibility suffers a complete collapse and his victims' wrath pours out on him in fullest measure.[77]

"Strangers," God's enemies by choice—people He never knew, "the terrible of the nations," will turn against Satan and abandon allegiance to his cause irrevocably.

"They have blown the trumpet, and made everyone ready, [b]ut no one goes to battle; [f]or My wrath is on all their multitude."[78] They "cut him

---

[76] Ezekiel 28:8,18, 19, NKJV.

[77] Rev. 20:10.

[78] Ezekiel 7:14, NKJV.

off"; they leave him; they are "gone down from his shadow and have left him" and "upon his ruin shall all the fowls of heaven remain...."[79] We know this is not literal scavenging, as there are likely no actual birds left.[80] The birds represent the cleansing action of the final fires (which we will get to in a minute) upon the remains of the wicked.[81]

At the great white throne judgment the books are opened and the wicked remember their sin.[82] It is burned into their memory as if written in letters of fire. Yet they have come to see and agree that God's ways are right. They can see clearly now that there is life only in Him, and only through obedience to His design principles that govern His creation can there be a secure and peaceful eternity. In the glorious light of His presence there is no longer any place to hide from the stark realities of truth about sin and righteousness. There is no longer any possibility of sin and righteousness co-existing. The righteousness of God's law, which is simply a revelation of His character of love, is now fully manifest to them, yet this manifestation only results in extreme torment. The full revelation of righteousness concurrent with the full revelation of sin produces an epic internal struggle which is said to "consume." Zechariah 5:4 speaks of the law in the midst of the "house" of the wicked, which will consume the timber and the stones.

The wicked will process their burden of sin to the cup's dregs, at last giving themselves over to it, at which point they beg God for the sweet release of death. Obadiah 1:16 says, "They shall drink, and they shall swallow down, and they shall be as though they had not been." The life force of the flesh will struggle hard against the idea of dying forever; hence, the weeping and gnashing of teeth. The mental agony will cause great physical stress as it did also in Christ, causing Him to sweat great drops of blood. But they will endure it until they reach the full extent of their capacity for pain and then finally give up the struggle, at which time they will be granted in mercy what they demand, the sweet release of death. "All they that hate me love death." "And death shall be chosen rather than life by all the residue of them that remain of this evil

---

79 Ezekiel 31:12, 13, KJV.

80 Jeremiah 4:25, 27.

81 Ezekiel 39:4, 6.

82 Proverbs 5:22; Ezekiel 36:31; Psalm 34:21; Revelation 20:12.

their lives; it is not the imposed will of God. Ezekiel 33:11 says, "[As] I live, saith the Lord God, I have no pleasure in the death of the wicked; but that the wicked turn from his way and live: turn ye, turn ye from your evil ways; for why will ye die, O house of Israel?"[84]

The Final Fire

The wicked see finally, that sin in the final act comes full circle and destroys itself. Sin itself destroys.[85] The lost have chosen to disconnect from God, their only Life-source. The everlasting burnings of the unquenchable fire of God's love do their sure work, yet without ever resorting to coercion or violence, and the wicked by their own choice perish in it. Their dead bodies, along with the elements, become fuel for the dissolving fire of fervent heat, the literal fire, the grand climax, when sin and sinners and all that has been corrupted by them will pass into oblivion. This is how Peter speaks of the fire of fervent heat that melts the elements.

> Looking for and hasting unto the coming of the day of God, wherein the heavens being on fire shall be dissolved, and the elements shall melt with fervent heat.[86]

> Every battle of the warrior is with confused noise, and garments rolled in blood; but this shall be with burning and fuel of fire.[87]

As the wicked fall by their own iniquity,[88] there is an accumulation of bodies over the face of the earth.[89] They go down in sorrow and weeping, yet admitting that God is just and fair in all His ways, clearing His name by assuming their own guilt. But they find it impossible to relate to Him as kind and gracious, the very thing needed to lead anyone to repen-

---

83 Proverbs 8:36, NKJV; Jeremiah 8:3; NKJV.

84 KJV.

85 Romans 6:23.

86 2 Peter 3:12, KJV.

87 Isaiah 9:5, KJV.

88 Psalm 94:23; 34:21; Ezekiel 11:21.

89 Jeremiah 8:2; 25:33; Isaiah 66:16, 24; Revelation 19:17, 18.

tance.[90] Jeremiah 49:5 speaks of the terror of soul that comes to those who are "driven out" by the wrath of God. That wrath is simply heaven giving them over to their choice not to have God in their lives. Therefore, because there is nothing left to show them that might still entice them to change their attitude towards God, there is no healing remedy left to cure their condition; there is no longer any possibility of repentance. At this point there is no one to mourn or gather up the dead.

As the wicked go to their deaths in the course of the "unquenchable fire" experience, God's hold loosens upon the fires within the earth, and violent eruptions begin breaking out everywhere. These fires Peter speaks of[91] as "reserved" or "kept in store" in the earth, in much the same way as the waters of old, in that they were upheld, sustained in place, by the Word of God. When that Word has jurisdiction only on the occupants of the "ark," —the Holy City, the restraint on the elements is removed and they now have no boundaries. They run their course, unfettered and furious, expending their energy. We could refer to these geophysical fires as the "fire reservoir."

At last, as the lost—both humans and angels—have expired and the earth begins to melt under volcanic eruptions and commences the transformation into one vast seething lake of fire, Satan is seen to be the last of the wicked left clinging stubbornly to life. His suffering will be the most intense, as the sins of the righteous have returned on his head with no one else left to blame.

It is just as depicted in the Sanctuary rite on the Day of Atonement. There is no place now for the Azazel scapegoat in heaven or on earth. As he looks around at the effects of his rebellion against God, all he sees is ruin and utter abandonment of his leadership. The Holy City is there now beginning to float on the sea of fire just as the ark of Noah once floated upon the waters of the great flood. That day long ago Satan had thought the world might end, but now he knows it for certain. He knows no possibility exists to escape this inferno and continue his work of rebellion and resistance, for there is no one left in the universe for him to deceive; therefore, he surrenders to the inevitable and, acknowledging his fate before God and the universe, willingly chooses to die.

---

[90] Romans 2:4.

[91] 2 Peter 3:5-7.

Just as Satan and his wicked host of angels originally found themselves without status in heaven and abandoned their estate,[92] so does Satan now go to eternal death, knowing that God's way is the only way that works. He now "leaves his estate" eternally with finality, for there is no place found for him in God's kingdom of love.[93]

The Fire of Fervent Heat

The final fire of physical decontamination Peter calls the fire of "fervent heat," in which the "elements melt."[94] It is the "fire from the midst," which comes out of the substance of creation.[95] It is the lake of fire at its climactic point, the dissolving fire,[96] the "smoke of their torment," which ascends "forever and ever."[97]

Not all elements melt in temperatures generated by common fires or even by the temperature of magma. Mere melting is not what is depicted.

There is an entire dissolution of the elements as they "pass away" with a "great noise,"[98] and ascend into smoke. They return to their basic condition of simple elements, returning the earth back to its pre-Genesis 1 condition of chaos. The only thing that can do this is a conversion of matter to energy, as seen in the chain reaction of a nuclear event. This is another kind of fire, a fire from the midst, a nuclear fire from the interior of matter itself. It is another kind of heat, a "fervent heat,"[99] beyond that of common natural processes.

Colossians 1:16, 17 and John 1:1-3 reveal that by the power of the Word of God—Jesus—all things are sustained and upheld. Now, at the point of final dissolution, that Word which was spoken, which made things to appear and to be sustained, is withdrawn and it is no more.[100] It is *ex nihilo* creation running in reverse. Everything that has been touched by

---

92 Jude 16.

93 Revelation 20:11.

94 2 Peter 3:10.

95 Jeremiah 48:45; Ezekiel 22:21, 31; 28:18.

96 2 Peter 3:11.

97 Revelation 14:11; Psalm 37:20.

98 2 Peter 3:10.

99 *Ibid.*

100 Psalm 33:6.

sin is now released from the sustaining Word of God, and it goes back into the void, where it has form no longer.

We see a harbinger of that final fire in the consuming of Elijah's altar.

> *Then the fire of the Lord fell, and consumed the burnt sacrifice, and the wood, and the stones, and the dust, and licked up the water that [was] in the trench.*[101]

That fire typifies the final dissolution of the elements. It has the sacrifice, typifying Christ. The observers have not yet committed their life to God; therefore, they may symbolize the lost. The bullock also symbolizes animal life. Plant life may be seen in the wood. The minerals of the earth are there, represented by the stones and dust. The water they diligently pour over the sacrifice typifies the waters on the earth. Even the atmosphere is burned up, for 2 Peter 3:10 says the heavens pass away with a great noise. Notice, please, no human being is burned alive by God's fire from the sky.

God will thereafter make His children a new home. "For, behold, I create new heavens and a new earth; and the former shall not be remembered, nor come into mind."[102]

> *And every creature which is in heaven, and on the earth, and under the earth, and such as are in the sea, and all that are in them, heard I saying, Blessing, and honor, and glory, and power, be unto Him that sitteth upon the throne and unto the Lamb forever and ever.*[104]

Eternity Begins

The war is over. The pain and misery which sin has caused is archived in heaven's history books at last. The scent of cleanliness and purity wafts through the universe to the highest star. The survivors' lives blend into the heavenly cadence to begin life everlasting in harmony with the principles

---

[101] 1 Kings 18:38, KJV.

[102] Isaiah 65:17, KJV.

[103] Revelation 5:13, KJV.

[104] John 17:23-24, WEB.

of love. From the Creator flows that life and light and gladness which they recognize, for it bore them up through their darkest days upon the earth. They lift up their voices eternally to praise Him, for they now know as they have never known before that God changes not. As never before, they know that God is love. Throughout ceaseless ages, the redeemed will thrive and glow with joy, for in their hearts there is no resistance to the love that fuels all creation. They have been healed, cleansed of all resistance to love and now they spend eternity ever increasing their capacity to live in joy and fellowship with the Godhead.

I in them, and you in me, that they may be perfected into one; that the world may know that you sent me, and loved them, even as you loved me. Father, I desire that they also whom you have given me be with me where I am, that they may see my glory, which you have given me, for you loved me before the foundation of the world.[105]

That which we have seen and heard we declare to you, that you also may have fellowship with us. Yes, and our fellowship is with the Father, and with his Son, Jesus Christ. And we write these things to you, that our joy may be fulfilled.[106]

---

[105] John 17:23-24, WEB.

[106] 1 John 1:3-4, WEB.

14

Jesus Bids Farewell

*"I still have many things to say to you, but you
cannot bear them now." (John 16:12, NRSV)*

Now it came to pass, when the time had come for Him to be
received up, that He steadfastly set His face to go to Jerusalem."[1]
When the disciples heard they were going to Jerusalem, they were
alarmed and confused—a condition they would not shake until after the
resurrection.

Why would He go to Jerusalem, they wondered. At Jerusalem the
envious scribes, pharisees, priests and other "saints" concentrated there
would likely kill Him and their own lives would be endangered.

Ah, ha! they reasoned. Maybe not. He would not be so foolish as to go
where they could impose control over Him and take His life. He must be
going to Jerusalem to take the throne of Israel! Finally He was going to
appear in His true character and show those wolves in sheep's clothing a
thing or two. As this new scenario sank in, they immediately began
disputing among themselves which of them would be the greatest in this
new kingdom; which one, in fact, would sit on His right hand and which
on His left.[2] The spirit of competition took hold of their minds, and they
could think of little else besides posturing for the most strategic position
possible where they could have the most power over the most people.

---

[1] Luke 9:51, NKJV.

[2] Matthew 18:1-4; 23:11; Mark 9:34; Luke 9:46; 22:24-26.

Therefore, while they, in keeping with their long-held national traditions, looked forward to earthly power and glory by expelling the hated Romans, what He saw ahead of Him was the sufferings of the cross. In spite of everything He taught them, their traditional beliefs made it difficult for the disciples to reach clarity. For three days after the Upper Room experience and the events that followed they lived in confusion and fear. They had always believed He was the Sent of God but now they felt uncertain. The trauma of these three days had rendered them, well, like driftwood on an endless sea. They were sure of nothing anymore.

They didn't understand, though He had tried to explain it to them so many times.They dreamed of earthly conquest through violence and force; He, on the other hand, was pursuing an eternal crown and a strategic victory far greater than anything His disciples could imagine.

They didn't understand that He was fully living out His own and His Father's character. There would be no sudden turn-around in His behavior. The story of His life on earth is filled with similar misunderstandings by many around Him.

Jesus' Last Talk With the Disciples
As the disciples entered the Upper Room on that last Passover evening, they saw nothing to distinguish this Passover from the many that had gone before. But Jesus knew that this Passover was different; this Passover was destined to be discussed down through the ages until the end of time. He must now bid *adieu* to His disciples.

Throughout that intimate discourse Jesus spoke of many themes, and though spoken directly to His disciples, Jesus intended those themes to be embraced by His followers down through the ages. He emphasized that we should love one another, especially our brothers and sisters of the household of faith. He said He had to go away for a season but we could count on His coming back after which we could be with Him forever. He gave us promises that would lift us above every challenge, and He informed us that we are His "friends." While we were servants for a season, now He calls us friends, because a servant isn't privy to the secrets of his master, while a friend is.

Then He said something that "sticks out" and I believe should have great relevance for us today. He said, "I still have many things to say to you, but you cannot bear them now. However, when He, the Spirit of truth has come, He will guide you into all truth."[3] What mysteries did He long to reveal? What truths did His soul want to impart? These secrets of the gospel have been unfolding throughout the seasons and years and millennia since Jesus departed and the cloud caught Him out of their sight. Since then, His everlasting light has been shining over the earth, shining on His friends and through them on the whole world, for "[T]he path of the just is as the shining light, [t]hat shineth more and more unto the perfect day."[4]

Jesus the Messiah

In that frame of mind, on the third day since the crucifixion two of the disciples set out on foot for a village called Emmaus. A stranger approached them, asking why they were so sad. Cleopas, one of the travelers, rehearsed the events of the last few days and shared that their hearts were broken by these events. The stranger then encouraged them with words of Scripture, providing clear evidence that Jesus was the long-expected Messiah and that He fulfilled every prophecy. This charged the men's hearts with joy. Arriving at their destination, the stranger appeared to be going on, but yielding to their entreaties, He went in and broke bread with them in Jesus' familiar way. The travelers then recognized Him as the Savior and saw that He was alive, to their everlasting joy and to that of the disciples at Jerusalem as well.[5] If they had been paying attention to Jesus just days before as they were traveling to Jerusalem, they would have known what to expect, and it would be reasonable to suppose that they would not have been so devastated when the crucifixion transpired. Jesus tried to tell them, but they were so caught up in worldly expectations that they didn't hear. Was this one of the "many things" that Jesus longed to impart which they were unable at that moment to comprehend? He tried many times to tell them what lay ahead of them in Jerusalem,[6] but the powerful attraction of their traditions blinded their eyes. In this case it was not the Holy Spirit but Jesus Himself who clarified what they had failed to understand previously when He spoke to them in the Upper Room.

---

[3] John 16:12, 13, NKJV.

[4] Proverbs 4:18, KJV.

[5] Luke 24:13-34.

[6] Matthew 20: 17-19; Mark 10:32-34; Luke 9:44; 18:31-34; John 2:19-21.

Obedience

There in the Upper Room where He said His goodbyes He also shared a new dimension of obedience. He spoke extensively about obedience, and notice, it was virtually always associated with our love for Him. He said, "If you love me, you will keep my commandments";[7] "They who have my commandments and keep them are those who love me";[8] and "If you keep my commandments, you will abide in my love, just as I have kept my Father's commandments and abide in his love."[9] No coercion here. He meant that when our love for God is real, when we see the demonstration of His own love for us, our hearts will melt with fervent love for Him, and the obedience, which may before have been burdensome because we expected it to lead us to heaven or enable us to escape hell, will become genuine and spontaneous, flowing out of us naturally. Abiding in His love; what joy! Knowing Him as He is lifts any burden of obedience. Loving Him, truly loving Him, always unfolds in true obedience, which is actually its natural fruit, not its root.

True as this is, obedience to God may yet have another motivation. If we choose the side of disobedience;if we do not find in true obedience our highest joy, God will,sadly and in keeping with His courtesy, release us to do whatever appeals to us besides His will for our good. We may prefer another god and, after years of calling us to Himself until His voice has faded from our hearing, He may have no choice but to admit that the god to whom we have shown preference has won the battle for our soul. In respect for our determined choice, He must then back off and no longer involve Himself in our affairs.

Throughout the years humanity has observed the principles of Karma,— "what goes around comes around." This is the universal principle of cause and effect that is alive and well and works everywhere. Scripture says, "[T]hey shall eat of the fruit of their own way/And be satiated with their own devices"[10] and "His own iniquities will capture the wicked/And he

---

[7] John 14:15, NRSV.

[8] John14:21, NRSV.

[9] John 15:10, NRSV.

[10] Proverbs 1:31, NASV.

will be held with the cords of his sin."[11]   Even the apostle Paul in the New Testament observed, Do not be deceived, God is not mocked; for whatever a man sows, this he will also reap. For the one who sows to his own flesh will from the flesh reap corruption, but the one who sows to the Spirit will from the Spirit reap eternal life."[12] This is describing one of the most fundamental principles of life, that choices result in outcomes consistent with what we have chosen. This is emphasized repeatedly in the Genesis 1 creation account when God says 'after its kind.'

God is our Protector. Through the ministry of holy angels and the Holy Spirit He guards us day and night. Our obedience is the pivotal choice whereby He is allowed to do this for us. Whom do we obey? God can and does protect us continually. "No weapon that is formed against you shall prosper, [a]nd every tongue which rises against you in judgment [y]ou shall condemn."[13] When we refuse to allow God full access in our lives and we turn our back on Him, well, He has no option then but to respect our rejection of His will and leave us to what we have chosen. But in doing so we also reject God's protection.

We can see how this paradigm might be viewed as sowing and reap-ing in the visible world.   When we happily go about our business in cheerful obedience to God, His agencies are there to protect us and to give us a good outcome. (Or the outcome that God sees best for us at the moment.) The Holy Spirit, in fact, working from within, gives us a new perspective that enables our victory. Scripture calls this the new birth. However,when we are content with the old nature, when we feel no need of God in our lives, we have little protection and, were it not for God's merciful grace, we would face the fiery darts of the enemy alone in keeping with the great conflict between God and Satan. Do you see how this view lends itself to belief in sowing and reaping?

If you do not see it now, perhaps you may see it in the future, when circumstances dictate that God must exercise His sovereignty in a straight line and no longer cover those who are His self-appointed enemies. Again, this is no fault of God. He loves all His children all the time, and His great heart of love grieves when we choose to go away from Him.

---

[11] Proverbs 5:22, NASV. See also Psalm 5:10; 7:15; 9:15, 16, etc.

[12] Galatians 67:7, 8, NASV.

[13] Isaiah 54:17, NKJV.

"Now by this we know that we know Him, if we keep His commandments. He who says, 'I know Him,' and does not keep His commandments, is a liar, and the truth is not in him. But whoever keeps His word, truly the love of God is perfected in him. By this we know that we are in Him. He who says he abides in Him ought himself also to walk just as He walked"[14] The apostle John didn't have our writing conventions to guide him in his day, and he gave a spin to his writings that sometimes sounds harsh to our twenty-first century ears. However, he got the message across, that if we truly love God, we will obey Him, and His love will flow spontaneously out from us.

Could Jesus not explicitly share this truth of obedience when He said goodbye to his disciples in the Upper Room just before his crucifixion, because they were not ready to receive it? Did the Holy Spirit design this message especially for us in the perilous times in which we now live?

The Holy Spirit

Jesus spoke extensively about the Holy Spirit's work on that last Passover evening with His disciples, stressing how vital is His presence in our experience. "He who has the Son [in the form of the Holy Spirit] has life"[15] The disciples understood that Jesus had something special to give them and were together in one place to receive it when the Holy Spirit fell on the day of Pentecost. It was the Gift of which Jesus spoke, saying, "I will ask the Father, and he will give you another Advocate to be with you forever. This is the Spirit of truth, whom the world cannot receive, because it neither sees him nor knows him. You know him, because he abides with you, and he will be in you,"[16] thus awakening them to the fact that the Gift would abide with them, in fact be "in them," and their hope of eternal life would depend on that connection.

Here we find the Holy Spirit enlarging our understanding of His own workings—vital knowledge for us in these latter days.

The Holy Spirit would assume responsibility for teaching the "many things" that Jesus could not impart to the disciples because they were not ready to receive it. "[T]he Advocate, the Holy Spirit, whom the Father will send in my name, will teach you everything, and remind you of all that I

---

[14] 1 John 2:3-6, NKJV.

[15] 1 John 5:12, NKJV.

[16] John 14:15, NRSV.

have said to you."[17] Could He have meant the subject of the character of God, as we have sought to unfold it in this work? In teaching this theme, He has called attention to many Scriptures that we have long overlooked, which we have used to share this exposé of God the Father. All over the world men and women are studying Scripture with new eyes and rejoicing as they see the Father in a beautiful new light.

The Revelation of God the Father
In the Upper Room Jesus spoke about His Father, the clearest representation of whom appears in Jesus' words in the gospels. I have reviewed these writings and pulled out the comments that contained any mention of His Father, and this is what I found.

John Mark (aka "Mark") wrote the first and oldest gospel, based on Simon Peter's memories. I can imagine him listening intently as Peter shared his memories of Jesus and sometimes badgering Peter with questions so as to make his account as accurate as possible, because Mark himself was not counted among the disciples. True, he may be found there,[18] but he was very young and leaned on his busy Uncle Peter for in-depth knowledge of the Incarnation. This probably accounts for the fact that he does not record Jesus' talking much about the Father. Mark began his gospel with the calling of the first four disciples, including Uncle Peter, very near the beginning of Jesus' public ministry. In fact, there are only about five references which mention the Father in any way in the book of Mark, and none of them speak about His character. Keep in mind Mark's limited contact with Jesus. It was easy to let the references to the Father fall by the wayside while recording the "important" events in the Master's life.

The gentile Doctor Luke was also not numbered among the original disciples and depended upon eye witnesses to provide context for the gospel he wrote to "most excellent Theophilus." But Christians through the ages have also read his stories, metaphors, and parables with delight. Although he records slightly more than Mark, Luke also shows Jesus making scant reference to the character of His Father.

---

[17] John 14:26, NRSV.

[18] possibly in Mark 14:51.

Two of the gospel writers, however, Matthew and John, were disciples, apostles, and eye witnesses to virtually everything that Jesus did and said, and they provide abundant evidence that arguably Jesus' favorite theme in everything He presented to the people was the paternal love and abundant graciousness of the Father. The former tax collector, Matthew, records Jesus' speaking about the Father some twenty-four times in his gospel, saying that the Father knows what you need even before you ask,[19] it is not the Father's will for anyone to be lost,[20] that children always have an audience with the Father,[21] and many other things that reveal the Father's true character. Truly, the tax collector Matthew transformed to "saint" as he followed Jesus during the years of His earthly ministry and partook of everything that Jesus said about the Father.

The gospel of the apostle John reveals the most about the Father. John was the youngest and longest lived of the apostles. He saw the literal destruction of Jerusalem in 70 A.D. that, when Jesus prophetically spoke of it so many years before, had filled his Master with such sorrow. John lived to see this prophecy literally fulfilled. Imprisoned on the isle of Patmos for the word of God and the testimony of Jesus, he "was in the spirit on the Lord's day"[22] and saw visions of God that would bless His church down through the ages until His return. Most relevant to our present theme however, he wrote of the great battle to take place at the end of time and emphasized that the dragon "was given" power and authority to wage war on the saints, and it was "allowed" to do certain things. Now we know why. The dragon receives power and authority to "wear out the saints,"[23] because of the great number of people who "buy" his lies, reflecting again the great war-in-heaven theme.

Matthew and John each have about the same number of references to the Father; that is, until readers get to John 13 wherein it virtually explodes with references about the Father. From chapter 13 to 17, which is Jesus' farewell to His disciples, I count another thirty-two specific refer-ences to the Father, making a grand total of about fifty-six such

---

[19] v. 18:8.

[20] v. 18:14.

[21] v.18:10.

[22] Revelation 1:10; Matthew 12:8; Mark 2:28; Isaiah 58:13.

[23] Daniel 7:25.

references in the book of John. Indeed, John considered this the heart and soul of his gospel and vital for the church to be aware of as it awaits Christ's return. Most of these chapters—13 through 17—illumine and inform us about the Father, and this focus is unpacked even more thoroughly in John's epistles later on, like an addendum attached to his original account.

Does God destroy? Did Jesus destroy—ever? Jesus emphasized that the Father is just like Him.

To make it plain, we might say that the Father *does* destroy. Scripture is clear on that. But when we ask, "*How* does God destroy?" —when we understand the dynamics of it, we would say from the human point of view that, like Jesus, He doesn't destroy at all. From our perspective we observe Him seeing and describing Himself as actually doing that which He only allows, when in reality human free will has denied Him the right to involve Himself in their affairs. Did Jesus have this truth in mind when He said, "I still have many things to say to you, but you cannot bear them now. However, when He, the Spirit of truth has come, He will guide you into all truth."[24]

The Point of the Story

The disciples who knew Him best, especially the one who not only knew Him best but loved Him longest, who long after Jesus had returned to heaven, when they presumably knew what His earthly life was about, emphasized that He reflected the Father.

> "For this reason the Jews were seeking all the more to kill him, because he was not only breaking the sabbath, but *was also calling God his own Father, thereby making himself equal to God.*"[25]

> "I can of myself do nothing. . . . I don't seek my own will, but the will of my Father who sent me."[26]

> "The Father and I are one."[27]

---

[24]John 16:12, 13, NKJV.

[25]John 5:18,NRSV, emphasis supplied.

[26] John 5:30, WEB.

[27] John 10:30, NRSV.

"An hour is coming when those who kill you will think that by doing so they are offering worship to God. And they will do this because *they have not known the Father* or me . . . because they do not know him who sent me."[28]

"Love your enemies and pray for those who persecute you, *so that you may be children of your Father in heaven*; for He makes his sun rise on the evil and on the good, and sends rain on the righteous and on the unrighteous."[29]

It has taken the world many wasted years to accept and internalize that Jesus reflected the Father. Why have we refused to listen? The cross of Christ makes a statement by which to measure all theories about the character of God. Jesus came to the earth largely to reveal the truth about His Father. God the Father is exactly like Jesus in every way. If the Father had appeared to us, His behavior and words would have matched the works and words of Jesus, for everything Jesus did and said was nothing but what He saw and heard from the Father. Seeing the similarity between Father and Son, we might have looked for another explanation for the "killing" language of Scripture. We could have worked it out from a careful reading of the word. Would not our overall character and that of the world have been the better for it?

"I still have many things to say to you, but you cannot bear them now. When the Spirit of truth comes, he will guide you into all truth."[29] Let us listen to the voice of the Spirit.[30]

"This is the message we have heard from him and proclaim to you, that God is light and in him there is no darkness at all. . . . [W]hen he is revealed, we will be like him, for we will see him as he is. And all who have this hope in him purify themselves, just as he is pure."[31]

---

[28] Matthew 5:44, 45, NRSV, emphasis supplied.

[29] John 16:12, 13, NRSV.

[30] Revelation 2:7, 11,17, 29; 3:6,13, 22..

[31] 1 John 1:5; 3:2, 3, NRSV.

BIBLIOGRAPHY

"A Curious Case of Sweating Blood." *Indian Journal of Dermatology*. 2009.

Allen, A. C. *The Skin: A Clinicopathological Treatise*. New York: Grune and Stratton, 2d ed. 1967.

Barbet, P. *A Doctor At Calvary: The Passion of Our Lord Jesus Christ As Described By a Surgeon*. Garden City, NY: Doubleday Image Books, 1953.

"Dead Sea." *World Book Encyclopedia*. 1954.

Barnett, Lincoln. *The Universe and Doctor Einstein*. Mineola, NY: Dover Publications, 1948.

Friesen, James G., Ph.D; E. James Wilder, Ph.D.; Anne M. Bierling, M.A.; Rick Koepcke, M.A.; Maribeth Poole, M.A. *The Life Model: Living From the Heart Jesus Gave You*. East Peoria, IL: Shepherd's House, Inc., 2004.

Foucher, Ray, https://characterofgod.org/2016/02/wrath-of-god/. 5/8/2018; https://characterofgod.org/2016/05/i-create-evil/. 5/8/2018.

Geikie, J. Cunningham, D. D. *The Life and Words of Jesus*. New York: D. Appleton, 1877.

"The Great Infidels." *The Works of Robert Ingersol In Twelve Volumes*. vol. III, The Dresden Publishing Company. 1881.

"Have Sodom and Gomorrah Been Found?" *Biblical Archeology Review*, September/October 2000, pp. 27-36; 300 Connecticut Avenue NW, Suite 300, Washington, D. C.

Holoubek, J. E. and A. B. Holoubek. "Blood, Sweat, and Fear: 'A Classification of Hematidrosis,'" *Journal of Medicine*, 1996, 27[3-4]:115-33.

Jamieson, Robert; A. R. Fausset and David Brown. *Commentary Critical and Explanatory On the Whole Bible*. 1871; rpt. Bellingham, WA, Faithlife, 1997.

Lea, Henry Charles. *A History of the Inquisition of the Middle Ages*. New York: Harper & Brothers, Franklin Square, 1887, 3 vols.

Lumpkin, R. "The Physical Sufferings of Christ." *Journal of Medical Association of Alabama*, 1978, 47:8-10.

Maglie, Roberto and Marzia Caproni. "A Case of Blood Sweating: Hematohidrosis Syndrome," *Canadian Medical Association Journal*, 23 October 2017, vol. 189, Issue 42.

Miller, Dave Ph.D. *Hematidrosis: Did Jesus Sweat Blood?* http//www.apologeticspress.org/APContent.aspx?category=11& article=1086, 7/6/2018.

Morris, H. M. *The Remarkable Record of Job*. Grand Rapids, MI: Baker Book House, 1988.

The New Strong's Exhaustive Concordance of the Bible. Nashville, Tennessee: Thomas Nelson Publishers, 1995.

Northrup, Bernard E. "On Finding An Ice Age Book." http:www.idolphin.org/iceage.html, 12/27/2017.

Paterson, Keith. "Where Was the Land of Uz?" https://biblereadingarcheology.com/tag/job/, 5/9/2018.

Samdahl, Don. http://www.Doctrine.org, 12/28/2017.

Setterfield, Barry. "Are Job and Jobab the Same Person?" www.setterfield.org/jobab.html, 12/27/2017.

Snelling, Andrew A. and Bodie Hodge. "Did the Continents Split Apart in the Days of Peleg?" http/www.AnswersInGenesis.org/geology/plate-techtonics/did-the-continents-split-apart-in-the-days-of-peleg, 12/27/2017.

"The Great Rift Valley." *Encyclopedia Americana*. 1983.

Sutton, R. L., Jr. *Diseases of the Skin*. St. Louis, MO: Mosby College
Publishing, 11th ed. 1956.

Trumbull, H. Clay. *Threshold Covenants or the Beginning of Religious Rites*.
Project Gutenberg. http://www.gutenberg.org/. 6/14/2015.

Wood, Bryant G. "The Discovery of the Sin Cities of Sodom and Gomorrah."
http://www.biblearchaeology.org/post/2008/04/The-Discovery-of-the-Sin-
Cities-of-Sodom-and-Gomorrah.aspx#Article. 2/27/2017.

www.ingramcontent.com/pod-product-compliance
Lightning Source LLC
Chambersburg PA
CBHW062214080426
42734CB00010B/1882